S0-AGZ-024

MISSION IN A DYNAMIC SOCIETY

J. ROSSEL

Mission in a Dynamic Society

SCM PRESS LTD

LONDON

Translated by J. G. Davies from J. Rossel
Mission dans une société dynamique
Labor et Fides, Geneva 1967

Footnotes especially written by the author for
this English version have been added, together with
further footnotes and appendices from the German edition
Dynamik der Hoffnung, Basileia Verlag, Basel 1967

SBN 334 01024 1

First published 1968
by SCM Press Ltd
56 Bloomsbury Street London WC1

© SCM Press Ltd 1968

Printed in Great Britain by
Western Printing Services Ltd Bristol

Contents

Introduction

THIS EXAMINATION of the role of the Church in a world in transformation by Dr Jacques Rossel is an important contribution to an on-going debate. This debate centres in a functional analysis of the Church; it is a discussion about what the Church is, not in ontological terms, but in relation to the society in which it is called to serve the purposes of God. Such a study must necessarily begin with the contemporary world, and this is precisely Dr Rossel's starting-point. He takes six places as paradigms: Bali, New York, Recife, Calcutta, Hong Kong and Mexico City. He describes these in detail and from this vivid account there emerges a number of characteristics of modern society: mobility, pluralism, the sense of the provisional, ceaseless change, revolutionary activity, secularization. Dr Rossel's presentation lifts these words out of the realm of vague generalization and clothes them with meaning and life. He thus enables the reader to appreciate the profound transformation that our world has undergone since the days of the closed medieval community. At the same time he assists us to appreciate our Christian opportunity and to recognize that we cannot proclaim the Gospel without initiating those who respond into their responsibilities in this complex situation. If the way to maturity used to be 'know thyself', the way to the fullness of the Church must involve also 'know thy social environment'.

Within this context of a dynamic society, no longer static but caught up in an irreversible movement, Dr Rossel defines the Church as a body which is summoned to join in the divine mission to the world. He warns against the danger of Christians becoming no more than do-gooders and tackles the question of the Christian message in relation to the situation he has analysed. He stresses the importance of taking the provisional seriously and discusses the forms, motives and organs of Christian witness. He contends that missionary presence is not simply physical, i.e. just being there, but must be at the same time a movement towards and on behalf of others, and he outlines what this means in terms of crossing frontiers, conversion and worship.

Dr Rossel steers a middle course between identifying all progress with the Kingdom of God and rejecting all that takes place in the world as irrelevant for salvation; he seeks an order within the disorder of the world and sees that order as the reality of the Kingdom which is 'already' but 'not yet'.

In his final section, Dr Rossel concentrates upon the western missionary in Africa, Asia and Latin America. He sets out the difficulties he has to face – the post-colonial situation, the view of the missionary as the envoy of an affluent society, etc. He demonstrates the need for the missionary to be a bridge between races and cultures.

Dr Rossel's study is both based upon and a constructive criticism of the ideas formulated by the Working Groups on 'The Missionary Structure of the Congregation' and by the Conference on 'Church and Society', both sponsored by the World Council of Churches. What he has to say is a judicious mixture of theology and sociology, and both balanced and illuminating. Not everyone will agree with everything he says – I do not myself – but I have no hesitation in commending it to English-speaking readers as a work that eschews extremism, which is theologically penetrating without losing clarity and is capable of holding one's interest and attention throughout.

The University   J. G. DAVIES
Birmingham

Our World

1 The Forward March

THE PUPILS of the Protestant secondary school at Bali in the Cameroons are lined up in classes on the large open square around which are arranged the various buildings of this boarding school. It is the morning inspection. Following this, three hundred boys in shorts and khaki shirts form a crocodile and advance, two by two, towards the hill. In front are the smallest, while the eldest bring up the rear. Soon they are passing in front of us. To the rhythm of their steps, our gazes cross. Then they enter into the chapel. The morning service, in English, is about to begin. The visitor has just time to rethink the short address he is to give to the boys. When the moment arrives, he speaks to them about Abraham:

'The march which you undertake every morning from your playground to this chapel is a symbol, an image of your life. When you left your village in the bush in order to come to a secondary school, you broke with one kind of existence; you set off on a march and you can never again come to a halt. When you go back to your villages, you will go either for holidays or as administrators, school masters, agriculturists, doctors or parsons; you will go as people who have been prepared for a new kind of life and who have decided to bring their villages into a movement which is irreversible. That movement began the very day that God said to Abraham: "Go from your country and your kindred and your father's house to the land that I will show you."'

But why are these children on the march? They would no doubt be quite incapable of saying. They would probably reply: 'In order to learn!' But where does their thirst for knowledge

come from? Why is it that every year more than a thousand
boys try to obtain a place in the school where only sixty can be
admitted? They have not received any precise call like that
which was addressed to Abraham.[1] What they have perceived
is entirely confused: the desire to join in the forward march of
Africa, about which news has reached their villages; their desire
for another form of existence which primary and biblical
teaching have opened up for them. But where are they going?
Perhaps the boys of Bali would reply: 'Towards a better
existence.' Now the call of Abraham is indeed a call to a better
existence: 'I will make of you a great nation, and I will bless
you, and make your name great, so that you will be a blessing.'[2]
To what degree will this new existence, in which boys from
thirteen to eighteen are engaged, be a source of blessing for
them, their families and their people?

This question is not primarily directed to these boys, whose
participation in this great forward march is no doubt more
emotional than reflective. It is directed first to those who are
responsible for the penetration into Africa of a new kind of life;
it is directed especially to those Christian missions whose
educational programme has been and still is, in many areas,
ahead of the African educative system; it is addressed to those
Christians who are supposed to know, not on a scientific basis
but by faith, that they possess in the bible an understanding of
the origin, meaning and goal of this forward march in which
they are themselves involved.

This question is also directed, with an ever-increasing sense of
urgency, to the Christian Churches of Africa, to their leaders,
and to the members they have brought up, who have accepted
the Gospel without always understanding the relationship
between its dynamism and the profound change through
which African society is passing at the present day. On the
one hand, the Churches are exerting great pressure on the
missionary societies, from which they sprang, to increase their
educational potential, both in terms of schools and of technology, and, on the other hand, they find themselves being

[1] Gen. 12.1ff.; cf. 11.31.   [2] Gen. 12.2.

left on one side by the ever-growing secularization which is the effect of the very education which is so much desired. Here is a contradiction and the reasons for it need to be examined.

Finally, this question is directed to us, to the European Christians, who often think that the end of the colonial era has set us free from a heavy responsibility. After having talked for four centuries of the white man's burden, we are now delighted to take sackcloth and ashes and to lament our ignoble past. As if to condemn the past is to make it better!

Where are these boys of Bali heading?

What is the meaning and what is the goal of the extraordinary march in which not only Africa and the countries of the Third World, but the whole world, finds itself involved?

One immediate answer to the question 'where are they going?' is both deceptively simple and down to earth. They are going to the city! In a few years' time we shall find them in Victoria, Buea, Bamenda, Douala or Yaoundé. The march in which today's world is involved seems to end up irresistibly in the city. So it is in Bombay that one can find the most active elements from the country and unindustrialized regions of the west coast of India. There comes a day when the intelligent worker declares: 'I am just vegetating here. I am going to Bombay where I can advance myself.' In Bombay, at the end of some ten years, he may be a foreman or even the head of a company. Alternatively, he may be discouraged and may cry out: 'Every season brings its new troubles here. War. Strikes. Caste or language disputes. There is no water to drink; there is no rice to eat. There are epidemics all the year round in Bombay. To eat, one must steal. Men harm themselves. There is no truth. Life is a lie; it is deceit, quarrelling and war. So why live? To fill one's belly. Three times a week in the restaurants rice is not served and instead the dishes are made with flour. In India at the present moment there is a scarcity of food. So why should we boast about ourselves? I have been in Bombay for ten years and I haven't yet found a room. I am disgusted with the struggle for survival. I have no longer anything to write home about. This is indeed the end of my letter. I beg you, without any desire for material things: Pray God for my health.'[1]

The city! It must be admitted that it is not very encouraging as the goal of the forward march in which the whole world is involved. When Indian evangelists retell the parable of the Prodigal Son, they describe the far country as a great city, as a place of dissipation. 'The son gathers together his portion and goes to Bombay. . . .' The city? It is often terrible; it is terrible for the majority of people. Nevertheless we must not forget that the bible employs the image of the city to describe not only the bankruptcy of human society but also its salvation. There are two cities that play an important role in the bible: Babylon and Jersualem. We are all of us inclined to see in our cities only Babylons and we disregard the promises of the heavenly Jerusalem. Indeed the bible uses the image of the city to refer to the goal of the long march which Abraham began: 'Therefore God is not ashamed to be called their God, for he has prepared for them a city.'[2] This promise should encourage us to deal more impartially with the phenomenon of our cities and to ask ourselves whether God is not at work within the political, religious and social transformations of which the cities are the laboratories.[3]

Indeed the great cities of our time have something to say to us. As we look at them, we have to acknowledge that they represent important stages in our forward march. In order to fulfil our Christian calling, we must pay attention to these stages. If we do not do so, we expose ourselves to dangerous illusions. We run the risk of wasting our time in rearguard action when our place should be out in front.

Of all the cities of the world today, it is New York that exercises a particular attraction. It is one of the most advanced stages in the forward march of the world. Let us then examine New York.

[1] Letter from Th.V., dated 1 December 1966, written in the language of the Canaries.
[2] Heb. 11.16.
[3] Harvey Cox, *The Secular City*, London and New York 1965.

2 New York, a Forward Stage in the Advance

New York is like a hazy mirror in which we may dimly find some hints about the meaning and direction of our forward march. Its skyscrapers are already invading the whole world. Whether this pleases us or not, it is a fact. Humanity in its totality is becoming more and more a tributary of a style of life, which for many reasons took shape in the United States (the New World!) and especially in New York. Isn't this irritating, disappointing, and even discouraging? Isn't it the proof that our civilization is in the process of going bankrupt? that this famous forward march is a march without meaning, quite capable of leading us straight to another Babylon? Quite a number of Christians can find this second Babylon in the hazy mirror of the modern metropolis. If New York really represents a stage on the road of progress, then would it not be better to march backwards, to empty our towns and repopulate our villages?

One of the things that strikes one first upon arrival by air in New York is the huge extent of suburbia, with its thousands of little houses, all the same and all arranged in squares, ellipses, circles or semicircles. The skyscrapers are only massed together in Manhattan, which is almost an island two or three miles wide and fifteen or so long and it is only a small part of Great New York, which is itself made up of an immense number of family residences. We know of course that in New York, as elsewhere, the centre is being emptied in favour of the outlying districts. Does this mean that the march backwards, to which we have referred, has already begun? It is highly improbable, since it is not a matter of returning to village dimensions. Indeed it indicates that the march is continuing. Manhattan, with its skyscrapers, is not a goal but a stage, and the outskirts of New York are yet another. This enables us to appreciate the first characteristic of New York, i.e. *movement*, of which one of the most spectacular expressions is the daily shuttling to and fro between the outskirts and Manhattan. This mobility appears to be at the very basis of the style of urban life.

In New York, even the stone, the reinforced concrete and the steel are conditioned by this movement. While urban centres as different as those of Paris or Berne give the impression of permanence, on account of their remarkable disposition, Manhattan, beginning with the statue of Liberty, is a medley of pinnacles and blocks of every height and shape. This lack of order is fascinating because it is beautiful and because it translates into steel and reinforced concrete the dynamism of the provisional which may well be the main characteristic of our period.

'In face of the increasing speed of all developments, a dynamic of the provisional, which leaves one freer the more one is faithful to what is essential, allows one to draw a fresh breath.'[1] What the Prior of Taizé is saying is directly relevant to the 'forward march', the meaning and stages of which we are trying to discover and understand. The most advanced stage – New York – seems to us the one most marked by the provisional. It is important for us to remember this fact and to be aware of the distance that separates New York from the cities of Europe, cities which have been orderly arranged for some six or seven centuries around their cathedrals. If New York had been built according to this model, the Empire State building would have had to be a cathedral. There is, however, no such thing. There are churches there – there are even many of them – but they are eclipsed by the skyscrapers. The great Roman Catholic cathedral of St Patrick, which was built a hundred years ago in the Gothic style after the model of Cologne cathedral, is a Lilliputian structure when seen from the roof of the Rockefeller Centre. At the advanced stage of our march, represented by New York, the church is removed from the centre of things, relegated apart and deprived of all its prestige, even when its tower reaches up to twenty-four floors, like that of the church of Riverside Drive on the banks of the Hudson. The Church is no longer, neither in stone nor spirit, the primary director of human life; it is no more than one element among others.

It is easy to understand why New York and almost all the

---

[1] R. Schutz, *Dynamique du provisoire*, Taizé 1965.

other cities in the new world have broken with the European tradition: even at the time of colonization, the conditions were no longer such as to permit the building of cathedrals. Confessional unity supported by ethnic unity was replaced by confessional and ethnic pluralism. The American colonists came from different confessions and different nationalities. There was no chance for them to unite their efforts in order to build a single cathedral in the centre of a new city. In any case, at least two would have been needed: one Protestant and one Catholic. The new world speeded the end of an era, that of the closed society, and New York reveals to us some of the consequences of this formidable transformation. Ethnic and religious pluralism demands the secularization of political and social structures, even of 'values' and morality, as well as the transformation of human relations and the creation of new methods of work.

So if we want to understand something about our world today, we must examine closely these facets of the contemporary open and mobile society.

3 A Closed Society and a Pluralist Society

Ethnic and religious pluralism means that a single centre of human control, as in Christian Byzantium or under Charlemagne, is replaced by several centres which have to achieve a minimum balance by means of a continuous effort. Despite Canossa, the religious and secular powers have become autonomous and so permit the creation of other centres of control.[1] The Empire has been dismissed into the realm of lost illusions and only rises again on the basis of a nihilist religion to create the ephemeral Third Reich.

In the natural man there is a nostalgia for unity. The Empire, of which we have just spoken, is only one of its expressions. Its most common expression is the tribe: one religion, one country, one head. It is the tribe that establishes the system of values and defines morality in relation to itself. Within the tribe everything is straightforward in so far as it conforms to its customs.

[1] T. van Leeuwen, *Christianity in World History*, London 1964, pp. 274-8.

Pluralism destroys all that. It establishes several centres of authority and several systems of values, in relation to which individuals are compelled to define themselves and to take their own decisions. The result is, on the one hand, an extraordinary liberation, and, on the other hand, disorder and confusion. Religious pluralism is revealed in New York by the fact that churches abound, but no single one can exercise a dominating influence over the others nor over the city in its entirety.

Ethnic pluralism defies description. As far as work and leisure pursuits are concerned there is a large measure of unity, but in terms of living accommodation there is complete disunity. In New York the only nationals that have been integrated are those from Europe; the rest live apart, in particular streets and particular neighbourhoods.[1] Man who is 'pluralist' in his work and leisure pursuits and whose life depends upon several centres of concern – firm, union, political party, religion, race, and family – becomes once again 'tribal' in his place of residence, and from this fact numerous tensions follow. The Bali boy who, when his education is completed, settles in Buea or Victoria, also finds himself in a similar, even if not identical, situation. All the African cities reflect the image of the pluralism of New York more than do those of Europe, for our cathedrals still link us with a past when the city was a unity, with a stage of the forward march which New York has passed and which the cities, whether ancient or modern, of Africa and Asia, as well as of Latin America, will also pass.

Ethnic and religious pluralism is only possible when the political and social structures have been secularized. To put this another way: these structures are no longer controlled by a single religious authority which is regarded as the source of all political and social life. In the Middle Ages the papacy considered that the Empire was dependent upon it. At Canossa, the emperor gave a visible demonstration of this. In actual fact, the independence of the Empire in relation to the papacy became

---

[1] Harvey Cox has stated that some large urban centres are divided into two sections which in fact represent two cities in one (*International Review of Missions*, LV, 1966, p. 274).

greater and greater. The 'temporal' became autonomous in relation to the 'spiritual'. This was the beginning of the process of secularization, of which the Reformation marked an important stage.

The immigrants into the New World, coming from religions, countries and languages, all of which were different, had to devise new political and social structures. No one religion could become the State religion; schools had to be laicized and toleration of religious differences was the indispensable basis of the new common life. At the same time the State wished to be neither a-religious nor anti-religious, and so allowed a place for God in the Constitution, without attempting to define his sphere exactly. It was in this way that there took place a certain integration of values and of morality which is still today at the basis of the 'American way of life'.

We shall return to the question of secularization later;[1] let us now pass on to another of the results of pluralism, i.e. the transformation of human relations and new methods of work.

In the village, whether it be the African village or the village of Europe in ages past, everyone knows everyone else and so relationships are durable and deep. Apart from some misfits whose nonconformity isolates them from any community, villagers do feel that they *belong* to the village family. This type of human relationship is no longer possible in the great urban centres. The more men are herded together, the more they become isolated. It is of course necessary to recognize that a degree of voluntary isolation is a defence of a person's right to privacy.[2] Yet this isolation means that the daily life of urban man becomes anonymous and casual. Personal relationships are no longer a given fact; they have to be created. They demand a choice by the individual citizen. By this choice he expresses his freedom, but this choice is at the same time the source of conflict and distress. It is possible to choose wrongly; it is possible, through fear of choosing wrongly, to make no choice at all and so to be submerged in complete isolation. The Bali boy

---

[1] See below, pp. 33–41.
[2] *Cf.* Cox, *The Secular City*, pp. 40–9.

when he arrives in Victoria must choose his relationships and select the group that will assist him in his choice. Had he remained in his village, this problem would not have arisen, since all he would have had to do would be to accept the choice determined by his tribal tradition.

Urban relationships have two dimensions; one of these is casual and anonymous, the other is selective. The Christian has to express his faith and bear witness in both. Now we have to admit that we have not hitherto thought about these questions sufficiently. We believe that our mission as Christians is to re-create in the city, street by street, both the mentality and surroundings of a village. This is a primary source of much of the confusion that is affecting the life of our churches in Europe and in Asia and Africa also.

Pluralist urban society also transforms the methods of work. The change-over from home crafts to work in a factory, controlled by a company which is largely anonymous, is a universal phenomenon. The stage represented by New York shows us the complexity of economic and social structures that can be produced by large urban centres. The order of the Middle Ages, which sought to integrate all the activities of life and to unite them with the ethnic and religious traditions, has been replaced by a multitude of organizations each of which concerns itself with a single narrowly limited section of economic or social life and at the same time attempts to be flexible and open to the future. Even when the organization is in the service of a religion or an ideology, it is usually pragmatic; it seeks to adapt itself to circumstances and it is assessed on the basis of results obtained. Caught up within the machinery of these organizations, the individual often feels out of his element and, on occasion, is just brutalized. He finds himself left behind by the multiple choices which these organizations impose upon him. At the same time, this very situation provides him with the opportunity to exercise greater freedom. He can select for himself his work, his factory or his office. He can change his work and he is able, by effort, study and know-how, to advance within the organization of his choice – unless he belongs to a section of the urban society which is deprived of this freedom of choice by the sheer necessity to keep alive.

Today's inhabitant of the city, because of the ethnic and religious pluralism, the secularization of the political and social structures and the transformation of both human relationships and the methods of work, has before him a greater range of choices than had his ancestor, who lived in a closed system. To choose, one must have a certain amount of knowledge and one must also be in a position to exercise one's judgment. But right judgment requires reference to a system of values and in the pluralist society there are several systems of values, and this both complicates matters and increases the chances of making a mistake. It is constantly being said that we live in a world that is fast becoming 'one world', and we are happy to emphasize the growing solidarity of mankind. But, at the same time, we have to recognize that in the realm of thought, we are as divided as ever.[1]

All this serves to show that the stage represented by the great conurbations is something of a pale reflection of that city of which God has laid the foundations! Indeed it represents an intermediary stage between three types of unity which we should distinguish from one another. Behind us there are closed cultures – European, African, Asiatic – which are being overtaken and broken up by urban pluralism. Ahead of us there are the two types of unity of which the bible speaks, represented by Babylon and Jerusalem.

Babylon stands for the application of the closed system of culture to the urban situation. Unity of thought, belief and action is obtained by joining in a common undertaking which exceeds what the individual can accomplish alone and is supported by an ideology imposed on all. The Babylon of Nebuchadrezzar and the Rome of Nero have both served as models up to the present day and will no doubt continue to do so.

Jerusalem is the image of the city 'which is bound firmly together'.[2] It represents a unity which is very different from

---

[1] *Man amid Change in World Affairs*, ed. L. J. Kramer, New York 1964, p. 43.
[2] Ps. 122.3.

that of the first two types, and we have to be familiar with it in order that our missionary witness may have direction.

New York represents a stage of extreme mobility among these different types of unity. The pluralism of its structures provides the men who live there with an extraordinary freedom coupled with a considerable responsibility, in view of the many and continuous choices that they have to make.

This pluralism, which is both the result and the condition of mobility, is spreading and it has already reached the majority of the cities throughout the world. Indeed it is also invading the countryside. One only has to cross the Swiss plateau to become aware of this. All this means that we have to prepare ourselves to take on the considerable responsibilities which a pluralist society lays upon individuals. It also means that we cannot announce the Gospel without at the same time helping those who accept it to face these responsibilities.

In a remarkable essay entitled 'Taille de l'homme', C. F. Ramuz has shed considerable light on some of the problems of today's world:

> Man only has stature in so far as he can still believe in himself; but he cannot believe in himself unless at the same time he believes in the existence of something which transcends him and presupposes him. . . . Man sees very well that when he makes an entirely spatial representation of himself, he is denying one half of his nature. He sees that there is no meaning except in eternity; for I love you, I also, O eternity, Nietzsche said. There are three ways of conceiving this: the Christian way which finds eternity in God; the physical way which absorbs the whole of the individual in the present moment; and finally the philosophical way which involves the infinite repetition of moments which are themselves transitory but necessarily recur. It is essential to realize that one can only love in eternity; that is why it is necessary to take care so to behave in every situation as if what one does were eternal.'[1]

So C. F. Ramuz declares that there are three ways of conceiving eternity; this is the result of the religious pluralism of our day. The temptation of pluralism is to refuse to make any choice. In relation to this W. A. Visser 't Hooft has written:

[1] *Œuvres complètes*, No. 16, Lausanne 1941, pp. 140f.

'Pluralism rightly understood creates for the Church a situation in which it is less in danger of falsifying its own nature and in which it is better able to manifest its true calling. Pluralism provides the Church with a God-given opportunity to live according to its own inherent spiritual law.'[1]

4 Gospel, Ancient Traditions and Modern Dynamism

At the time of the great missionary conference at Tambaram, near Madras, in 1938, there were two different conceptions of missionary method. The one recommended the regrouping of those newly baptized into special villages or neighbourhoods, in such a way that they could lead a social life bearing the imprint of the Gospel. The other conception was opposed to this; it was held that a new Christian should remain within his own *milieu* and that its structures and customs should be respected. Neither of these methods took account of the evolution of society towards pluralism. The first took its point of departure from the idea that Christian villages, with some sort of 'theocratic' structure, could exist in isolation without degeneration; the second one rested on the idea that if the Gospel were sown in the soil of a particular culture, it would develop all the positive characteristics of that culture without being alienated from it. The hopes that were placed in the first method have not been realized. As for the second, Roger Mehl has written:

Every attempt at indigenization raises a difficult problem: the rooting of Christianity in an indigenous mentality and culture presupposes that Christianity will find themes and ideas in the religion or indigenous culture which it may after a manner baptize, and that the religion or indigenous culture will serve as a basis for a Christian construction, it being interpreted as a religion which Christianity may bring to fruition and fulfilment. But there is little evidence to support such a hypothesis.[2]

[1] 'Pluralism – Temptation or Opportunity', *Ecumenical Review*, XVIII, 1966, p. 145.
[2] *Décolonisation et missions protestantes*, Paris 1964, p. 77.

The wrongness of transplanting our ways of behaving, our theological questions and forms of thought, our music and our architecture has been very fully described.[1] It is time that we took note of the fact that indigenization has been more radical in certain respects than has thitherto appeared. 'Acculturization', to use a current term, is a complex phenomenon. The number of local customs which have been consciously or unconsciously assimilated into the life of the Churches, established by the missionary endeavour, is probably much greater than the number of those imported. Yet the adoption of certain customs confronts the Church with some difficult problems when these customs are attacked by the social revolution; this is the case with caste or tribal divisions, with dowries and marriage contracts. Customs that are sanctioned or tolerated by the Church assume a quasi-sacred character which it is very difficult to remove. Of course the transplantation of European customs to Africa or Asia is ridiculous, but it is equally ridiculous for a Church to perpetuate social customs which have become outmoded, or even to defend them, as was the case with the dowry in Kerala.

The supporters of indigenization, like those of the 'Christian villages', took no notice and indeed still appear to take no notice of the fact that our world is in movement and that therefore all customs, European or indigenous, are transitory. Rather than staying in the past, we must prepare to face the future. When the reports of the Tambaram Conference (1938) are read and compared with those of the Mexico Conference (1963), it is immediately apparent that, within twenty-five years, the vision of the world has radically altered.[2] It is no longer static; it is dynamic.

The radical wing at Tambaram, while acknowledging that the Gospel both changes and transforms things, believed that it was possible to dissociate artistic techniques (music, dance and culture) from the religion of a place and to preserve them within a new culture transformed by the Gospel, a culture whose

[1] J. Rossel, *Découverte de la Mission*, Neuchâtel 1945, pp. 149ff.
[2] J. Rossel, 'Tambaram-Mexico', *Evangelisches Mission-Magazin*, 4, 1964.

continuity would then be assured. There was to be a kind of
transubstantiation of culture in its entirety. Hence the central
temple on the island of Bali should have become the principal
sanctuary of the Bali Church. The style of the doorways would
remain unchanged, but the subjects of the sculpture would be
altered: instead of guardian demons, there would be the four
evangelists. The womenfolk would have filled their baskets
with offerings as in the past. Within the courtyard, the bas-
reliefs dedicated to the Hindu epics would be redone to present
the biblical history. In the centre, beneath a great thatched roof,
men and women in national costumes would have taken
communion with rice and palm wine. Songs, supplications and
prayers would have been accompanied by traditional instruments.[1]

In order to realize this dream, it would have been necessary
for everyone on the island to accept the Gospel. But even where
missionaries have made efforts to lead a whole people to the
Gospel, as among the Nagas in North India, the Karens of
Burma, the Bataks of Sumatra and the Papuans of Australian
New Guinea, there were defections and certain tribes and
families refused to embrace the new religion. This is the first
obstacle to a complete and effective transubstantiation. The
second obstacle arises from the fact that the era of closed or even
semi-closed civilizations is past. The homogeneous tribe is now
only one of the elements that make up the *nation*. The concept of
the nation, imported from Europe (but applied without the
ethnic base which is to be found in Europe: the French nation,
the German nation), has been imposed in Africa and in Asia, as
it was a century ago in Latin America. Decolonization has
simply provided it with a new strength. While the colonial
powers, with the possible exception of the French and Portuguese, favoured the development of tribes in isolation, the new
states are concerned with centralization. So there is the struggle
to integrate Katanga with the Congo, the Nagas in India, the
Karens in Burma, and the Bataks in Indonesia. This struggle is a
matter of life and death as far as these new states are concerned,

[1] *idem.*, *Découverte de la Mission*, pp. 164–9.

since a federation, like that in Switzerland before 1848, would make them vulnerable and would encourage the intervention of neighbouring powers and possibly lead to their own dissolution. Decolonization does not allow these liberated people to forge new links with their past but forces them to develop new structures which are adapted to the economic and social needs of the present. Hence in India the distinction between the castes has been abolished and this was something the British never dared to attempt. It has even set about reforming the Hindu law of succession, which again the British were careful to leave untouched, and this is leading to the disappearance of 'joint families' and to the creation of smaller family units. Moreover, in India today the women have obtained a position of equality with the men which, at least in politics, goes much further than anything to be found in the most developed Western nations. K. M. Panikkar, the historian, who is not exactly sympathetic towards the West, believes that certain contributions from the colonial period are absolutely necessary for those nations who have undergone decolonization: 'There is no doubt, therefore, that the changes that have been brought about in Asian life by the contact with Europe are radical and far-reaching, and will not disappear as many observers are inclined to think with the rise of a new Asian sentiment. It would be useful at this point to examine the major features where Western influences are likely to be permanent, and the extent of these influences on Asian societies in general.'[1] On the following pages Panikkar lists first among the principal items the question of law. 'In all Asian countries the legal systems have been fundamentally changed and reorganized according to the post-revolutionary conceptions of nineteenth-century Europe.'[2] One of the greatest changes is the recognition of the equality of all citizens before the law. In India in former times, according to Hindu teaching, a Brahmin could not be condemned on the testimony of a Sudra, and similarly, according to Mohammedan ideas, a believer could not be judged on evidence supplied by a non-

[1] *Asia and Western Dominance*, 6th impression, London 1965, p. 324.
[2] *ibid., loc. cit.*

Mohammedan. Another considerable change relates to the position of women. He then considers forms of government, the nature of political law, democracy in the widest sense of the term, the new metropolis, the national State, modern science and scientific thought. According to Panikkar there is nothing, not even language, which has not undergone profound alterations. 'Philosophy and religious thinking, however much they may influence the people in general, are the special interests of the intellectuals. But not so the language, and it is here that the influence of Europe has been most noticeable. . . . Today in China the forms of writing which are followed show little or no influence of the classics, and are modelled upon the literature of the West.'[1]

This great Indian historian, who is the former Prime Minister of a maharajah and Ambassador of India in Peking, Cairo and Paris, completes his list by referring to the ecumenical conscience, in the secular sense of the term, i.e. to the sense of belonging to one world and not being a world apart. Nevertheless it is to be noted that Panikkar also believes firmly in the continuation of the Asiatic civilizations. In his study *Hindu Society at the Cross Roads* (1965), he invites his co-religionists to accept the profound changes that the new national life will bring and he is convinced that Hinduism will be capable of assimilating them. He is able to be an optimist because he believes that in his country the social conscience is in advance of social practice and that high-caste Hindus have done more than others towards the transformation of the nation.

The final page of *Asia and Western Dominance* is one of the most interesting. Panikkar holds that Europe has not sought to impose an ideology on the Asiatic people. Indeed 'the influence of the contacts between Asia and Europe is not wholly one-sided and, since the political domination of Asia is a thing of the past, the results of the interpenetration of culture may be even more fruitful'.[2]

According to Panikkar, it is the Asiatics themselves who, in order to resist Europe, have learned from it the necessary

[1] *ibid.*, p. 329.   [2] *ibid.*, p. 332.

techniques so that they can fight it with their own weapons. General T. B. Simatupang of Indonesia argues along the same lines. He explains that the impact of the forces originating in the modern West is such that the fundamental likeness of its effects is more noticeable than the differences, and he continues: 'It has been the common experience of the colonial peoples that all their efforts to liberate themselves from western colonialism, often motivated by a spirit of genuine heroism, failed as long as they faced the modern West with their traditional art of warfare and with their traditional methods of organizing society. Only after they had absorbed or borrowed enough elements of the spiritual, scientific and material revolution that had transformed Western man and Western society into modernity were the non-Western nations able to set themselves free.'[1]

We must take very seriously these statements that emanate from those of whose love for their people and their culture there can be no doubt.[2] They allow us to appreciate that decolonization is not the restoration of a *status quo* but a new move forward. Twenty years of decolonization prove that this move can be both radical and fast. In fact this move relates to a revolution on the spiritual, scientific and material levels, and the elements of this have been quite deliberately borrowed from the West. Of course, nationalist propaganda emphasizes the cultural treasures of the past; ancient names are restored to honour, ancient customs re-established, and Western civilization, and Christianity with it, are severely criticized. Twenty years after its independence, India is being shaken by a crisis of religious orthodoxy the results of which are unforeseeable. There is a considerable effort to rediscover the living sources of the past. Everywhere museums are being opened. The newness of structures is often represented as no more than the renaissance of ancient ones which had been forgotten. The work of artists in the East owes much to primitive art. Quite a number of

---

[1] *Responsible Government in a Revolutionary Age*, ed. Z. K. Matthews, London and New York 1966, p. 171. (This is Vol. II of the 'Church and Society' Conference preparatory studies.)

[2] Similar statements have been made by Africans; cf. *Tradition et modernisme en Afrique noire*, Paris 1965, pp. 31ff., 53ff.

Westerners are contributing to this current of ideas which is the normal corollary of decolonization. The day will come when it will be recognized that all this relates, far more than one realizes at present, to a projection backwards of new ideas into the pre-colonial times, just as at the Renaissance there was a projection of new ideas back into Antiquity or as in nineteenth-century Switzerland revolutionary ideas were read back into the legendary history of William Tell! This dichotomy between the new ideas which are transforming the structures of an ancient society and the folklore with which they are often associated could be dangerous, because it carries with it the risk of obscuring the real problem raised by the evolution of closed societies, whether European, Asiatic or African, towards pluralist societies.[1] We may be helped to appreciate this problem in its true dimensions by our consideration of the New World. There is, in a museum in Washington, a section devoted to the various cultural contributions out of which the pluralism of the United States has been formed. Here is displayed the evidence of contributions from England, Italy, France, Spain, Germany, Holland and Scandinavia.[2] All of this means that pluralism is not a creation *ex nihilo* and that there is continuity between the past and the present.

While accepting the movement towards pluralism, we must also seek to safeguard our rich inheritance from the past. Pluralist society is not necessarily colourless; on the contrary, its pluralism should allow it to unify the extraordinary richness of creation.[3]

The problem of *acculturization* should be examined again. There must be a middle term between a radicalism which holds

---

[1] One of the most disturbing examples is Japan; *cf.* Ernst Benz, *Asiatische-Begegnungen*, Düsseldorf-Cologne 1963.

[2] There is no Swiss contribution, for the simple reason that Switzerland is pluralist.

[3] 'God seems to love variety as much as man seems to love uniformity. Variety is not to be treasured for its own sake. Yet it would be a strange thing if the various races of humanity did not have peculiar treasures to bring into the Kingdom of God' (S. Neill, *Colonialism and Christian Missions*, London 1966, p. 420).

that the new times separate us for ever from the past and a conservatism which deliberately ignores the evolution which mankind is undergoing. But this middle term is not simply a formula. It must be embodied in a style of life. We believe that this style is the one to which the Gospel is summoning mankind. Between a radicalism that may issue in nihilism and a conservatism that may produce an apartheid of universal proportions, there is the mission of the Christian Church, a mission which is fulfilled under the cross and by faith in the promises of the resurrection of Christ and of his Kingdom which is to come.[1]

5 Intermediary Stages

Recife

Recife is the capital of the north-east region of Brazil and its development is encountering the same difficulties as other regions throughout the world. In spite of having more than a million inhabitants, Recife is still a pre-urban agglomeration. Around the core of the ancient city, which goes back to the beginning of the Portuguese settlement, there are grouped residential districts and poor neighbourhoods, as well as *favelas*[2] which are situated in the low-lying part and are subject to regular flooding.

In the course of a seminar, consisting of some sixty leaders of the professions from different denominations, on the subject of

---

[1] Hence we dissociate ourselves from a theology of mission that may be called 'transubstantianist' or 'integrist'; a notable example of this is provided by Kaj Baago, Professor of Church History in the United Theological College, Bangalore. 'The missionary task of today cannot be to draw men out of their religions into another religion, but rather to leave Christianity (the organized religion) and go inside Hinduism and Buddhism, accepting these religions as one's own, in so far as they do not conflict with Christ, and regarding them as the presupposition, the background and the framework of the Christian gospel in Asia. Such a mission will not lead to the progress of Christianity or the organized Church, but it might lead to the creation of Hindu Christianity or Buddhist Christianity' ('The Postcolonial Crisis of Missions', *International Review of Missions*, LV, 1966, pp. 331f.).

[2] A Latin-American word for 'shanty towns'.

family planning, which is especially vital in a city growing as rapidly as Recife (16 per cent each year), a Brazilian doctor, who is a member of the regional parliament, made the apposite observation that the primary problem for Brazil, which is largely uninhabited, is not the control of the birth rate but the proper use of the land and the creation of new opportunities for work.

The government team, which is responsible for the development of the north-east region, is young and dynamic. Alphabetization, hygiene and professional training are the necessary factors leading to industrial development and urbanization. A huge campaign of alphabetization, in which a Presbyterian Church has taken the initiative, is strongly supported by the government and also receives encouragement from other Protestant Churches and even the Roman Catholic Church. Groups of all ages, from fourteen upwards, have been formed in the night schools and these are then put in charge of alphabetization classes, which are held from 7 to 9 o'clock every evening in all suitable places—churches, schools, shops, etc. These classes are composed of students of all ages. It is not unusual to meet a grandmother with her grandchildren. The lessons are concentrated within a certain number of weeks. These are followed, for the better students, by other courses which provide them with a primary training. In the near future these will be also followed by classes for elementary professional training, thus helping the labourers to become semi-skilled workers. This phase of the immense programme is the most difficult because it requires exact co-ordination with the existing industries and the development of new ones.

Through this great campaign, hundreds of instructors from very different backgrounds are coming into direct contact with the inhabitants of the poorest districts. There are ultra-conservative Protestants, who have been hesitant to recognize that social work is a part of Christian witness; there are Catholics, too, who have been conservative also for social and political reasons, and they have given up their mutual distrust to collaborate in a task the consequences of which cannot but be considerable, since alphabetization opens new horizons, extends an invitation to a better future and arouses hope that must be satisfied.

Another noticeable feature of this campaign is the method adopted to prepare the way for it. Although the hope is to reach all members of the population who are illiterate, there is no predetermined plan. Those districts chosen for alphabetization are selected because they show an interest in it. First of all the natural leaders of these districts are sought out and the purpose of the campaign is explained to them so that they can talk to others around them. When a majority of these leaders are in favour and are ready to co-operate with the organizers the campaign is launched in their district. In this way one of the primary conditions of development is ensured: the active participation of those who are going to benefit. The Roman Catholic Archbishop of Recife, who is one of the most alive among the South American episcopate to the Church's responsibility within a society which must develop quickly to survive, is never tired of repeating that development can never bear fruit unless those whom one wants to affect join in from the beginning. A development imposed upon others cannot succeed. Underlying this development, there is a spiritual problem. First of all the inner powers of man must be set free so that he may be directed towards a life in which he is ready to engage to the limit of his capacities and even beyond. Of course not everyone answers this call. But it has to be addressed to all so that some may respond and draw the others along with them.

The Benedictines, who have been settled in Recife for four hundred years, have provided land for those who live in the *favelas* so that they may build solid and hygienic houses. This only concerns some twenty houses at the moment. A very simple plan, identical for each house, has been devised. Site clearing has been undertaken with the help of the beneficiaries, who have been chosen by the social agencies. They have to make their own bricks with the sand and cement provided and they build the walls of the houses themselves. Some are almost complete, one is already inhabited. Men are to be seen carrying bricks and building the walls of the next one. The project is advancing slowly as the people concerned have little free time and are not properly qualified for this kind of work. Further, the question of drainage has not yet been settled, and so the Benedictines are not forcing the pace.

The Recife stage provides us with several important items of information which are applicable to all urban developments. Development must be undertaken on two levels at once: the level of common action on a wide scale (the alphabetization campaign) and the level of limited objectives (the Benedictine project and those of other organizations like the YWCA which have not been mentioned). Each level is essential and the Church should join in both. To put it another way: Christian service has two dimensions, a social dimension and a personal one.

Traditional Christian service is from person to person, like the service rendered by the Good Samaritan (Luke 10.25ff.). In a patriarchal society, this kind of service would be all that is necessary, but it becomes entirely insufficient within an industrialized and pluralist society where the problems are presented on a totally different scale. It is necessary for the State, i.e. the collectivity, to intervene, to organize and to regulate. Hence the State takes charge of education and the health services, which the Church was almost alone in undertaking prior to the advent of modern society. The Church, through its members, joins in this immense task, which is the duty of society at large, and it should do so joyfully, recognizing that this collective social work is a form of service. 'To the extent that the State, even when it is completely secularized and separated from the Church, attempts to assist and ensure the social well-being of the individual and of the community within a lawful structure which is not totalitarian, the believer ought to see it as a servant of God with the same aims in the social and political field as the Church itself.'[1]

Nevertheless, person to person service has not lost its importance. However socially advanced a state may be, it is never

[1] A. Rich, *Die Weltlichkeit des Glaubens. Diakonie im Horizont der Säkularisierung*, Zürich 1966, p. 64.

paradise. There will always be misfits. 'The failures, the aged, the handicapped, the misfits of all ages, with their tendency to new forms of crime, need above all persons who take them to heart and who support·them unconditionally without allowing anyone to fall by the wayside. If the social state (*sozialer Rechtsstaat*) cannot find people who are ready to perform this person to person service (*mitmenschlicher Dienst*), it would soon find itself, for internal reasons, faced with an untenable situation.'[1]

These two dimensions of Christian service are complementary – the social dimension regulated by the norms fixed by the State for the well-being of the whole community, and the personal dimension with limited objectives. The Church, as a body of believers, must see to it that this complementary character of the two dimensions is preserved, and, in so doing, it will exercise a critical function, indeed a prophetic role of the greatest importance. 'By community service (*gesellschaftliche Diakonie*), the Church is made aware of its joint responsibility within the political and social structures of the world and has to keep watch to see that they are really serving human existence (*Mitmenschlichkeit des Daseins*), and this involves the changing of the structures if they become inhuman. Here is a new and vital task for which we must acquire a clear vision.'[2]

The Conference on 'Church and Society', which was held at Geneva in July 1966, set itself the task of acquiring this clear vision by examining with care the political, economic and cultural problems which present themselves to the world within which the Church has to make its act of witness.[3]

[1] *ibid.*, p. 66.   [2] *ibid.*, p. 76.

[3] *Cf.* R. Mehl, 'The Basis of Christian Social Ethics' in *Christian Social Ethics in a Changing World*, ed. John C. Bennett (Vol. I of the 'Church and Society' Conference preparatory studies), London and New York 1966, pp. 44–58; also, by the same author, *Traité de sociologie du protestantisme*, Neuchâtel-Paris 1966, pp. 275ff.

Calcutta

Calcutta is the largest industrial city in India and indeed in the whole of south-east Asia. The success of its industry is also the cause of its difficulties, because it draws crowds from the countryside where they can no longer make a living. So the problems which have to be faced in Recife are being repeated in Calcutta on a huge scale. Nevertheless, the most striking thing about Calcutta is the contrast between an amorphous society, which is fatalist and capable of periodic acts of violence, and a dynamic society, consisting of those who have passed through the secondary schools, the universities and the technical colleges, upon whom depends the development of the metropolis and, with it, an entire section of the nation.

Many observers have described the painful impression created by the journey from Dum-Dum airport, which is situated on the outskirts of the city, to the centre of Calcutta. The least important thing is the dilapidated condition of the bus; at least it runs and, after the wastage he has seen elsewhere, the traveller appreciates even this measure of economy. But he is disagreeably surprised by the ill repair of the road, the obstruction of the open drainage channels and the dirty water which spreads everywhere. Hundreds of idle people, poorly dressed, fill the streets. Here is a shopkeeper with his blind hanging on a single hinge, and he has neither the energy nor the knowledge to repair it. Here is another floundering daily in dirty water which floods out of the channels in front of his stall and he makes no attempt whatsoever to improve the situation. Yet often all that is needed is a blow with a pick or the use of a spade. But perhaps they have neither a pick nor a spade, and then, why bother as long as one's neighbour will not do the same? Passivity, indifference, resignation. Only what is strictly necessary for existence is actually done. It is claimed that in Madras only 25 per cent of the population at an age to work is involved in a productive activity. The remaining 75 per cent depends for its existence upon a thousand small intermediate employees, which is the accompaniment of a poor economy, where retail sales are subdivided to such an extent that even a boot lace, a razor blade, half a cigarette, a quarter of a candle or a finger of oil are resold because a large part of the population cannot afford to buy more at a time.

The journey from the airport to the hotel, which lasts about an hour, by the light of the electric lamps in the streets and of the oil lamps and candles that illuminate the shops, is both disillusioning and depressing. Where can one start to improve only a little the conditions under which these crowds of resigned human beings pass their lives? At Recife a priest has settled in the midst of a *favela* with no resources other than those of the people whose life he has come to share. Yet it is too early to say if his presence will bring power or will be simply tolerated as a curiosity.

One Sunday, we went to the huge sports ground near the cathedral in the centre of Calcutta. It was about nine o'clock in the morning. The sight is quite extraordinary. Everywhere groups of college and university students are at play, some at cricket. Their dress is impeccable; their shirts have been newly washed and ironed; the trousers belonging to the older ones, and even the shorts worn by the youngest, have their creases well defined. The majority of these young folk belong to the small middle class and have to struggle constantly to reach the end of their studies. On the Saturday evening, dressed in old shorts and sleeveless shirts, they had pressed their own shirts and trousers with a heavy charcoal iron so that they could take part in the Sunday cricket; the most privileged among them had done this in their rooms in college, the others heaped together with their families in one or two rooms.

Others had spent their Saturday evening starching their National Cadet Corps uniforms. On that Sunday there were to be seen everywhere groups of cadets – and even cadettes – with their instructors, each sporting a beret with a red pompon, and drilling between games of cricket. One could feel their concentration, their determination to prepare themselves, as much internally as externally, to defend their country. Yet this willingness to prepare for defence, expressed in the form of an antiquated drill, was almost comforting, despite the horrors of war which it evoked, after the apathy of the crowds through which we had passed the previous night on the road from the airport.

If the alphabetization campaign in Recife does not achieve at least some of its objectives, then, in a few years, this Brazilian metropolis will be like Calcutta. It will be a vast agglomeration composed of amorphous masses, incapable of doing for themselves whatever is needed for their own development, and over against these a small group of élite consisting of young folk full of energy spending themselves to improve a little the conditions of their existence and of those of their families, and it is upon these that finally depends the development of the whole nation. This disproportion between these two sections of society is terrifying. It would indeed be dispiriting if there were not a light of hope in the eyes of these young people, which is a kind of reflection of a vision of a better world which has seized them and will not let them go.

Hong Kong

The confused mass of refugees in Hong Kong differs in no way from the dwellers in the *favelas* of Recife or the districts of Calcutta. There is the same herding together, the same economic situation (it is even possible that they sell matches one by one in Hong Kong!), and yet the traveller is favourably impressed by the fact that the inhabitants and the public authorities are struggling together to improve the living conditions in this city which, in twenty years, has increased its population from half a million to four million on a very restricted area of land. The refugees are rehoused in blocks of seven or more floors, and even if two hundred people per floor have to use the same conveniences, all this is a considerable advance upon their previous situation and ensures at least a minimum of hygiene for them. The city administration is not afraid to overcome obstacles. Hills are removed, valleys filled in, and at the same time business and industry are developed, and this allows an increasing number of people to engage in productive work. But the administration would be powerless without the help of the population. The Chinese is an extraordinary being; for him work is a religion. Because of this he has little difficulty in accommodating himself to the rhythm of the modern world. If you go into a Chinese shop to buy a toothbrush, you will have hardly mentioned your need before a boy of six will be busying himself to find what you want. The Japanese are the same. The film *The Naked Island* evokes quite remarkably a furious devotion to work which is quite out of proportion to the result obtained.[1] Here is the great difference between the Western and the Chinese understanding of work. These two concepts are meeting in Hong Kong and this is perhaps the reason why that city gives the impression of facing up to its problems.

Mexico

With its six million inhabitants, Mexico is the largest city in Latin America. It owes something to New York, Recife, Calcutta, and Hong Kong. Here one finds all the problems of conurbation. We refer to it here because it is in the midst of a country which is proud of its precolonial past, a country which ignores three hundred years of Spanish rule and which is always telling the visitor that it has had every kind of revolution that has affected the Western world. The Mexicans have even built a museum dedicated to the last 150 years of its history. This museum, shaped like a spiral, is on the hill of Chapultepec, close to the scene of the drama of Maximilian. One enters from the top and going down a gentle slope one is presented with a series of dioramas, with spoken commentary, which trace the main stages of Mexican history since decolonization. There is no escaping the recognition that political independence is not a final goal but a point of departure.

The independent Empire (1822) was followed after a year by a presidential republic that was both conservative and clerical. There followed years of humiliation, with the loss of New Mexico and California, sold to the United States, and a long

[1] *Cf.* Benz, *op. cit.*, pp. 27-46 for his description of the volcanic island of Sakurashima.

civil war from which Juares, the first president and of pure Indian descent, emerged victorious. He secularized the Church's property and deprived it of a large part of its influence. Next came the foreign intervention and the fiasco of the shortlived Empire under Maximilian of Austria, created and supported by France, and then the return to power of Juares. Finally, in 1911 and 1917 (February!) there took place the peasant and workers' revolutions which put an end to the great estates and to the most flagrant abuses of industrial capitalism. Because of all this Mexico is almost a hundred years in advance of most of the other Latin-American republics and for thirty years has had sufficient political stability to develop a flourishing economy, thanks to a determined policy of nationalization, which is at the same time sufficiently flexible to attract foreign industries. Although it is the neighbour of the most powerful nation in the world, to whom it had to cede some hundred years ago a large amount of land, it has been able to preserve both its political and economic independence and its cultural originality which attracts thousands of tourists every year.

The stage which Mexico represents should allow us to understand a statement made by the Japanese Professor Takenaka at the first Christian Conference in East Asia in 1959. He remarked that Asia had to go through, in a brief span of time, the same six revolutions that the West underwent from 1517 to 1917: 1. The spiritual revolution of the Reformation; 2. The industrial revolution; 3. The American anti-colonial revolution; 4. The French Revolution with its charter of the rights of man; 5. The racial relations revolution that culminated in the American war of secession; 6. The proletarian revolution of 1917. Professor Takenaka concluded: 'It is no exaggeration to say that the six revolutions that took place in the West over the last four hundred years are all happening at once in Asia.'[1]

Mexico accomplished these six revolutions in less than 150

[1] *Witnesses Together* (Report of the East Asia Christian Conference), 1959, p. 34, quoted in *A Factual Study of Asia* (Report of the Commission on Ecumenical Missions and Relations of the Presbyterian Church in the USA), 1963, p. 156. See also Simatupang, *art. cit.*

years. Those states that are the result of decolonization will not have so much time to undergo this. It is this telescoping of six revolutions into a very short period of time, on an unprecedented scale, that gives our epoch its special revolutionary character.

6 The West and its Revolutions

Certain questions are raised by the example of Mexico, and the statements of Professor Takenaka and General Simatupang of Indonesia. Why are these revolutions necessary? From whence do they derive their all but universal character? Why did they first take place in the West? It is not easy to answer these questions. Several theologians have made the attempt;[1] the conference on 'Church and Society' in Geneva in July 1966 concerned itself with them[2] and Paul Hazard has devoted an important study to these problems.[3] Yet clarity has not yet been achieved. It is more than probable that agreement will not be reached either about what is essential or about the details. Nevertheless, our action is determined by our answers to these questions, whether we admit them or not and whether we are conscious of it or not. But these answers are often very incoherent. We are afraid to appear neo-colonialist by discovering something good in Western civilization, even if it is only in its revolutions! Yet at the same time there is great stress on the need for a social revolution on a world scale. Western civilization is declared to be pagan in principles and aims and, with the same breath, we laud secularization as its most distinctive achievement as if it were the Kingdom of God! There is enthusiasm for neo-Hinduism and Zen Buddhism and yet the structure of the world to come is discerned in urban pluralist

[1] F. Gogarten, *Verhängnis und Hoffnung der Neuzeit*, Stuttgart 1953, 1958; D. von Oppen, *Das personale Zeitalter*, Gellhausen-Stuttgart 1965; K. H. Miskotte, *When the Gods are Silent*, London 1967; T. van Leeuwen, *Christianity in World History*; H. J. Schulz, *Conversion to the World*, London and New York 1967; H. Cox, *The Secular City*; R. Mehl, *Traité de sociologie du protestantisme*, section on the Reformation, pp. 275ff.

[2] See the Reports.

[3] *La crise de la conscience européenne*, Paris 1964.

society. It is surely time to straighten out our ideas even if this involves upsetting certain habits of thought. Decolonization is now some twenty years old; it has been achieved despite some reactionaries – it should now be possible to demythologize it. Every revolution has its myths and decolonization is no exception; they are probably necessary, but the time comes when in order to move forward they must be left behind. The Reformation of the sixteenth century also had its myths, in particular that which turned the pope into the Antichrist, and this has been very tenacious. It is possible that the myth that Western civilization has been responsible for all past, present and future evils will be equally tenacious. We cannot overcome this concept in isolation; we must have the help of our brothers in Africa, Asia and Latin America. It is they who must tell us why they reject Western civilization except for its revolutions and why they maintain this distinction within Western history when the majority of our Western contemporaries are incapable of so doing. It is time for us to examine in depth this distinction instinctively drawn by our Latin-American, Asian and African brothers between our civilization, which they reject, and our revolutions, which they regard as necessary; if we do this, we may discover the way out of the confusion in which we are at present.

On the basis of this distinction, which is common among the representatives of those nations that have recently been decolonized, we should accept the concept of *accidental acquisition* and use this in our thinking about civilizations and cultures. We are required to distinguish between a given civilization and certain acquisitions to which it has given currency; these acquisitions are not to be regarded as an intrinsic part of the civilization nor as a necessary extension of it. Let us now try to grasp this concept more clearly by examining one of the effects of the Western revolutions, viz. secularization, beginning with a definition of revolution itself. The first thing to note is that the primary meaning of revolution is very different from its figurative sense. In astronomy, geometry and mechanics a revolution is a rotatory movement around an axis; hence it refers to a circular movement. According to its figurative use, however, revolution refers to a sudden, violent and irreversible change which effects a break in continuity.

It should be noted further that the Conference on 'Church and Society' had great difficulty in defining revolution in a way that was acceptable to both the representatives of the West and of the Third World.[1] The Western delegates were inclined to see in the phenomenon a speeded-up evolution rather than a succession of convulsions or ruptures. André Philip, who cannot be accused of conservatism, maintained that in modern industrial society there is no longer any possibility of sudden revolution. The continuous revolution, in which that society is involved, is more a process of evolution than of sudden and violent irruption. The delegates from the Third World, on the other hand, were compelled by their own circumstances to emphasize the sudden and violent nature of the revolution which they are undergoing.

These two views can be united if attention is paid to the different situations of those who put them forward. While the Westerners have had more than four hundred years to absorb the six revolutions listed by Professor Takenaka, and more than a century to assimilate the one that was most violent, i.e. the French Revolution, as well as recovering from the passionate romanticism which accompanied it, the inhabitants of the Third World are experiencing them all together and are unable to distinguish one from the other. Decolonization has scarcely come to an end before they are thrust into the industrial revolution. The need for individual freedom comes into conflict with the necessity for a strong régime. Tribal, linguistic or religious allegiances threaten the unity of the nation. The social revolution is under way. While in the West we have the remote consequences of former revolutions, the Third World is the scene of unco-ordinated disturbances. In the West there is a diluted and controllable process of revolution, while in the Third

---

[1] A. Rich, 'La révolution, un problème théologique' (Appendix to the fourth item on the agenda of the Extraordinary Assembly of the Federation of Protestant Churches of Switzerland, 1966, pp. 4ff.).

World there is revolution in its pure state, concentrated and hence difficult to control and both sudden and violent.

It is probably necessary to give up trying to distinguish precisely between evolution and revolution. It is easy to be a supporter of evolution when one is the beneficiary of a long series of revolutions; but it is quite understandable that people should be against evolution when it is necessary to make up a great deal of lost ground for which they have not been responsible. In any case, neither evolution nor revolution is to be found in its pure state; the two are intermingled. There are periods of rapid advance and of change which can properly be termed periods of revolutions, but there are others which appear to be much calmer; the one derives from the other. Preparation for revolution takes place in a period which is apparently peaceful, and the revolution, in its turn, inaugurates an era of stabilization. Evolution and revolution can be united if it is recognized that both are part of an irreversible movement which dominates both. In this situation what is needed is not a theology of evolution nor of revolution, but a theology of movement or mobility.

In this study the word revolution will be employed as a correlative of evolution and vice versa; in this way it is hoped to circumvent a debate which in the last analysis is likely to be futile. Defined in this way, revolution includes not only the political reality but also the sciences, technology, the community as a whole and the realm of the spirit.

7 Secularization[1]

One of the most noticeable effects of the Western revolutions is secularization. In itself secularization is not a Western phenomenon. Periods of secularization, of differing lengths, have been

[1] 'Secularization in Western Europe started way back before the Reformation and has been among us ever since, always gathering momentum, always becoming closer to the people, always eating away at the authority of the church' (Albert H. van den Heuvel, *The Humiliation of the Church*, London and Philadelphia 1966, p. 16). The entire chapter 'Secularization as Freedom and Yoke', from which this quotation is taken, gives a good

experienced in Greek, Hindu and Chinese civilizations; but their effects were not commensurable with those in Western civilization because the causes were not the same. At the basis of the Western type of secularization there were a certain number of revolutions.

The first revolution to be noted is that in the conception of work. Unfortunately this subject has not yet been studied in depth.[1] To appreciate its origins we probably have to go back to the period before the establishment of the cities of the late Middle Ages – cities which became active centres of the new concept of work – to the founding of the Benedictine monasteries with their motto *ora et labora*. The Benedictines, by their example, invested manual work with a moral value, whereas previously it had been regarded as a laborious task fit only for slaves. It is indeed striking that even writing and the education of children were regarded as inferior tasks to be left to intelligent slaves.[2] This concept was missing from the thought of Judaism. The prosperity of the Jewish *diaspora* in the Roman Empire was in part due to the fact that the Jews did not disdain to work with their own hands, as may be proved by the evidence of St Paul.[3] This revolution in the concept of work found a home in the monasteries of the West and from there passed to the cities founded in the Middle Ages. The Calvinistic Reformation – there is general agreement on this – contributed to the elevation of work to the dignity of a kind of lay ministry and this served to increase the prosperity of those areas in Europe which received

account of recent research into and discussion about secularization. See, too, Hermann Lübbe, *Sekularisierung, Geschichte eines ideenpolitischen Begriffs*, Freiburg-München 1965. Lübbe's study gives a valuable account of the concept of secularization in France, Germany and the Anglo-Saxon world. See Appendix 3.

[1] Professor L. Joubert mentions this in his address to the Conference of European Churches at Nyberg, 1964, and Professor von Oppen touches upon it in *Das personale Zeitalter*.

[2] See Plato's *Gorgias* quoted in *Theologisches Wörterbuch zum Neuen Testament*, ed. G. Kittel, Stuttgart 1933ff., II, p. 81. Hereafter referred to as TWNT. (The English version now being prepared and translated by G. W. Bromiley, Grand Rapids, Mich. 1964ff., has virtually the same pagination.)

[3] Acts 20.33f.; I Cor. 4.12; Eph. 4.28; I Thess. 4.11.

Huguenot refugees after the revocation of the Edict of Nantes in 1685. Work, conceived as a ministry, then became for a large number of people a kind of cult as well as a source of profit. But this latter perversion does not allow us to doubt the evangelical value of the revolution in the understanding of work, nor to deny the influence it has had upon secularization. The Western concept of work is in fact based upon the idea of the desacralization of things and this leads to what Professor Joubert has called 'the autonomy of the profane'.[1]

A second revolution which played a considerable part in the phenomenon of secularization is that which was revealed in the investiture controversy. It is usual to see in this only a struggle for power between Church and Empire, but this power struggle not only complicates the historical situation but also obscures the fact that at its basis there were two overlapping revolutions – a revolution of the Church against the Empire and of the Empire against the Church. It is important to recognize that the Church in the Middle Ages, in struggling for its autonomy against the Empire, succeeded in maintaining a bipolarity, a certain tension between the functions of the Church and those of the State. In the East there were similar struggles for Church independence over against the Empire but the outcome of these was schism and the progressive loss by the Empire of those areas that became schismatic. In the West, the Church managed to preserve a certain degree of autonomy over against the State.[2] The result of this conflict, in the West, was the creation of two almost autonomous spheres which henceforth continued to exist side by side.[3]

The Reformation, in the name of a rediscovered biblical faith, declares that secularization is necessary. This spiritual revolution, to give it Professor Takenaka's title, is one of the major contributors to the phenomenon of secularization. Hence the

[1] *Zusammenleben als Kontinente und Generationen*, Nyborg IV, 1964, p. 108.

[2] The Roman Catholic Church achieved this with greater ease than those Churches that emanate from the Reformation, because the structures of the latter were, and are, exclusively regional.

[3] For further details see T. van Leeuwen, *Christianity in World History*, pp. 282–8.

need to dwell on this at some length. The Reformation attaches great importance to the struggle of the prophets and of Jesus against the sacralization of people and things. According to Isaiah: 'Bring no more vain offerings' (1.13), 'learn to do good; seek justice, correct oppression; defend the fatherless, plead for the widow' (1.17). Does not secularization begin here? The cultus, which consists of vain offerings and observances of all kinds (1.13f.) and is aimed at the sacralization of things, seasons, actions and of those who perform them, is to be replaced with a cultus in spirit and in truth which transforms the relations with the oppressed, the orphan and the widow. It is impossible to be more radical! Jeremiah takes up again this essential distinction: 'Do not trust in these deceptive words: This is the temple of the Lord, the temple of the Lord, the temple of the Lord. For if you truly amend your ways and your doings, if you truly execute justice one with another, if you do not oppress the alien, the fatherless or the widow . . . then I will let you dwell in this place' (7.4–7). There are then no sacred places, no sacred stones; certain elements of the creation cannot be isolated and declared holy in distinction from the rest that remain profane. The whole of creation is 'profane' simply because it is creation. Jesus endorsed this prophetic message. Of the Temple, he declared: 'There will not be left here one stone upon another' (13.2). According to his teaching all things are pure (Mark 7). It is true that he drove the merchants out of the Temple, but this is because they were growing rich by selling offerings and vain sacrifices, whereas the only function of the Temple is to be a house of prayer (Mark 11.15–19). The Sermon on the Mount (Matt. 5–7) is really a treatise on secularization. Alms, prayer and fasting are deprived of everything that gives them a sacred character. By returning to the preaching both of the prophets and of Jesus, the Reformation began a spiritual revolution and the consequences of this are still with us today.[1]

[1] '. . . *the story of the self-disclosure of JHWH, the revelation of JHWH, is not only secular but also secularizing.* It has been pointed out repeatedly that revelation of God is a secular action; it means that even in the pre-scientific

The Renaissance equally encouraged in its way secularization. The autonomy of thought, literature and the arts was affirmed by returning to the forgotten pagan myths of Greek and Roman antiquity.

The classicism of the seventeenth century put a brake on this movement by creating a synthesis between the autonomy of the Church and the autonomy of the age on the basis of a static pre-Copernican conception of the world. Paul Hazard has demonstrated how behind this apparently peaceful façade a split was developing of which the West and with it the entire world is still undergoing the positive and the negative results. Its way paved by a revolution in the concept of work, brought into the open by the investiture controversy, demanded by the Reformation and supported by the Renaissance, secularization found its philosophical expression in the empiricism of John Locke which differed in spirit so much from the geometry of Descartes. While Descartes, according to Fontenelle,[1] sought to penetrate to the source of everything and to master primary principles by means of certain clear and fundamental ideas from which the phenomena of nature would appear as necessary corollaries, Locke repudiated metaphysics. 'His aim was to make truth his only goal and to attain it by careful examination, without living off alms, without resting on the opinions of others, without caring if he could claim the authority of a Plato or an Aristotle, and without necessarily approving the words of his masters.'[2] This spirit of careful examination is characteristic of the orientation of the new thinking. Nevertheless, this spirit is not

language of the Bible the holy merges with the profane and so produces the secular. The *shalom* of God . . . (which includes all earthly things such as justice, and good, and peace, and freedom, and righteousness) is given and measured in social and political categories and has only transcendent qualities in this way. Whatever you say about what happens in the Bible between Israel and JHWH, and between Jesus and Israel, the pagans and the nations, it is clear that the Bible uses very secular language. It does that to such an extent that Biblical literature – literarily speaking – has much less standing than many other religious writings, and catches the divine 'incoming' into this world in political, social and secular terms' (van den Heuvel, *op. cit.*, p. 40).

[1] Quoted by Hazard, *op. cit.*, p. 294. [2] *ibid.*, p. 223.

simply the will to be independent, it is also the will to humility, for it was resolved to examine only what is capable of being examined, and the first things to examine are the possibilities and limits of our understanding.[1] It would, however, be a mistake to assume that because of this concentration upon the things that are within our understanding Locke was a sceptic. He defended himself against charges of materialism or even of deism. This Protestant philosopher, exiled in Holland and returning to England with William of Orange, considered himself to be a Christian and he knew how to distinguish between faith and reason. Reason enables 'the discovery of the certainty or probability of such propositions or truths, which the mind arrives at by deduction made from such ideas which it has got by the use of its natural faculties, viz. by sensation and reflection'. Faith is 'the assent to any proposition, not thus made out by the deductions of reason, upon the credit of the proposer, as coming from God in some extraordinary way of communication. This way of discovering truths to men, we call revelation.'[2]

With the empiricism of John Locke, applied by Newton to physics, by Grotius to law, and by Bayle to morals, there began a revolution, the way for which had been paved by other revolutions concerning work, the relations of Church and State and the relations between faith and religious tradition; the consequence of this has been a progressive secularization of the

[1] Hazard sums up Locke's position in this way: 'The certainty which we need is in our own soul: let us then contemplate our own souls and turn our gaze away from the infinite spaces which just produce mirages. Let us concentrate our attention, knowing that our understanding is limited but also accepting the necessary limits; let us analyse it within these limits and come to appreciate its functions. Let us observe the way in which we form our ideas and how they are held together; let us consider the way in which our memories preserve these ideas; all this is an immense undertaking that we have hitherto neglected. It is here that we shall find true knowledge, the only one which is sure. The perspectives are so great that our life is too short to contemplate them all' (*op. cit.*, p. 226). There is also this sentence by Locke himself, taken from the preface to *An Essay Concerning Human Understanding*, 1690: 'Our business here is not to know all things, but those which concern our conduct.'

[2] *An Essay Concerning Human Understanding*, IV xviii 2.

structures of life and this has promoted the pluralist society of our day.

The French Revolution provided these successive revolutions with a political and social structure. During the one and a half centuries that followed it, more things happened in the West than during all the 1500 years which had gone before – an era of a millennium and a half which began when the emperor Constantine made Christianity the state religion. Since the French Revolution, we have witnessed the separated worlds of nations and cultures giving place to a single world, more and more closely united as far as its technical, economic, political and social structures are concerned – this is our world.

The revolutions which we have just passed in rapid review have only an accidental character in relation to Western civilization. It does not seem possible to maintain that they are the logical consequences of their cultural antecedents, the roots of which extend into the civilizations of Greece and Rome. Such a conclusion would appear to support the often heard statement that Western civilization is pagan in both its beginnings and its end.

If, however, these revolutions are accidents, we still need to know what produced them. In our view a major part in this must be assigned to the preaching of the Gospel. This preaching in the West has never entirely lost its prophetic character. It was nourished both by the prophetic teaching in the Old Testament and its fulfilment in Jesus Christ. While the 'saints' of the Eastern Church were more mystics than prophets, the 'saints' of the Western Church were more prophets than mystics.[1] This prophetic movement culminated in the Reformation of the six-

---

[1] N. A. Nissiotis has denied the truth of an over-facile distinction between the Eastern and Western monastic ideal. 'To regard Eastern mystical theology only as a negative spiritual power for social action is to ignore its main characteristic, which is to be found in the creative dynamism of the regenerating power of the Holy Spirit. True monasticism gives life to the people of God, pointing at the same time to the end of history and to the second coming of Jesus, when he will meet his own people. Monasticism is the missionary church going out into the world, possessing nothing, being a living witness to the second coming of the Lord' (*Christian Social Ethics in a Changing World*, p. 79).

teenth century and with the Renaissance opened the way for the unfettered research of the philosophers and the men of science.

The main characteristic of the prophetic message is to insist, in season and out of season, on the essential distinction between the Creator and the creature, for the message of salvation or reconciliation cannot be understood apart from this distinction. The biblical view of the world is based upon this distinction, while the pagan view is concerned to eradicate it and even to deny it. To pagan man the temple is holy; to the prophets and Jesus Christ it is not so. The pagan draws a distinction between sacred and profane; Jesus did not do so. The only distinction there is to make is that between the Creator and the creature. This prophetic distinction sets man free, whereas the pagan distinction between sacred and profane gives rise to superstition and to magic which then enslave man.[1] Wherever this freedom is proclaimed, there the vision of man changes, as it is directed towards the possibilities inherent in this liberation and so becomes dynamic. The revolutions listed by the Japanese professor are continuous expressions of this. But all these

[1] Many examples can be cited; we shall restrict ourselves to one, viz. the traditional customs of the Dajaks on the island of Kalimantan in Indonesia. The director of a Swiss agricultural college who has visited the island reports as follows: 'With technological backwardness we must also include difficulties of a spiritual kind. The whole life and thought of the Dajak of the hinterland are dominated by fear of gods and demons to whom they must offer continual sacrifice. To this must be added numerous taboos – objects that are not to be used or areas which must be avoided. This narrowness due to pagan animist religion is a serious obstacle to human development and to the use of new methods of agriculture.' In reference to the undertaking at Tumbang Lahang, he says: 'The newly undertaken work is threatened by a number of things. Pagan sorcerers are trying to discredit the agricultural college in the eyes of the populace. If a village is struck by illness, this is laid to the charge of the college. It is the revenge of the devils because they have not received sufficient honour or have not been brought enough offerings. Yet all these curses and spells are not preventing the development of the college. Another stage of culture is emerging as a small village is built near the agricultural college in which a joyful group of students enter into contact with the science of agronomy' (W. Sommerauer, *Aide aux jeunes paysans Dajaks*, *Mandat sans Frontières*, Geneva 1965, pp. 137ff.). This was published shortly before the violent death of the agricultural engineer, André Stuby; the true causes of this are still unknown.

revolutions have made their appearance within Western civilization, which is at bottom pagan, and hence they have an ambi-
valent character. They have been undertaken both for better
and for worse; they have set men free and they have subjected
them to new forms of slavery.

8 An Essay in Interpretation

Although this ambivalence must be stressed, it need not prevent
us from recognizing prophetic elements in these revolutions. It is
indeed these very elements that have ensured their vitality more
than their radicalism. Today we are in agreement with our
Roman Catholic brothers and condemn the radicalism of the
Reformation, which is still being experienced in a number of
ways in our day, e.g. the violence between Protestants and
Catholics in Belfast in the summer of 1966; we are also in
agreement about the importance for the whole Church of the
prophetic elements in the Reformation.[1]

The many gains which have been secured through these
revolutions during the history of the West are *accidental*. These
accidents are understood by the believing Christian, at least in
part, as the outcome of the apostolic proclamation. It is the
Gospel which gives work its right place. It is the Gospel which
sets faith free from human traditions. It is the Gospel which
fights against those superstitions that fetter man in the accom-
plishment of his task, which consists in serving and in loving.
It is the Gospel which requires us to look into the heart of man
and not at the accident of his birth. It is the Gospel which
requires us to bear one another's burdens.

All this, it is necessary to repeat, concerns the Christian
believer.[2] To use Locke's terms, it is a matter of assenting to a

---

[1] *Ecclesia in via pergrinans vocatur a Christo ad hanc perenam reformationem qua
ipsa, qua humanum terrarumque institutum, perpetuo indiget* (Decree on Ecumeni-
city, II. 6). 'The Church in its pilgrimage is called by Christ to a continuous
reformation, which she always needs, in so far as she is a human and earthly
institution.'

[2] 'The theologians, after having overcome their initial fear of the phenomenon of secularization, have discovered that the Christian faith itself has

proposition which is not based upon the deductions of reason and can never be. It would be equally impossible to base a contrary argument upon reason. All that the empiricist can affirm is that these revolutions have taken place and that they are accidental, i.e. they have no necessary connexion with the antecedents of the civilization within which they have appeared, and that they have been produced by a host of very different factors between which it is extremely difficult to make any choice. The Christian believer chooses in virtue of his faith; that is his right. There are of course non-Christian believers who choose in virtue of *their* faith. We have to examine their choice to understand their attitude and their reaction and also to illuminate our own choice.

We have quoted K. M. Panikkar above. All the adherents of neo-Hinduism believe with him that it is possible to unite with Hinduism all the gains resulting from the Western revolutions without changing it in its basic structure, because, in their view, these revolutions are culturally speaking *neutral*. It may seem that our concept of 'accidental acquisition' provides them with some support. But if they are neutral, as far as culture is concerned, are they also from the point of view of religion? They answer this question in the affirmative. It is *their* choice made in virtue of *their* faith. There are quite a number of Europeans, including convinced Christians, who are in agreement with them. We must take account of this and consider its consequences.

If these acquisitions or gains are neutral, not only from the

a secularizing function. Nothing liberates people from the control of powers and principalities more than the gospel itself. We now know that without the preaching of the strange freedom in Christ, secularization in Europe would not have taken place; it is not accidental that secularization got hold of people in a Christianity-permeated culture. The Christian faith secularizes in that it frees people from all other powers, so man and his community can really decide whether they want this particular God or not, whether they want to go their own ways and to live independently, or whether they want to follow the way indicated and taken by the Messiah of Israel' (van den Heuvel, *op. cit.*, p. 86). The author adds a question mark to the expression 'the world we know', because this knowledge cannot be acquired only empirically but presupposes a certain faith in the Gospel itself.

cultural but also from the religious point of view, and if the
'Western' gains are simple techniques, divorced from any
questions of origin or goal, then the revolutions which have
produced them cannot have the importance that is usually
attributed to them at the present day.[1] Their effects last just
as long as is needed for the pond to return to its calm after
having thrown a stone into it. They only appear to be new and
they have no definite effect upon the development of our world.
Basically, despite what may be said to the contrary, there would
appear to be only one possible view of the world and only one
possible faith, which can be expressed in a single sentence:
Everything is in everything else, and there is nothing that is
new. Hence, having devoted more than 400 pages to a careful
study of the profound changes which have turned the West from
a static society into a dynamic one, P. Hazard concludes:
'Everything is in everything else. *We know this*;[2] there is nothing
that is new.'[3] He skilfully leaves the final word to Leibniz:

[1] This seems to be the position of Roger Mehl in *Décolonisation et Mission*.
'Certainly one cannot speak today of an absolute decline of Western
civilization. Under one of its forms at least it has conquered the world. It has
conquered in so far as it is a civilization of work and technology. The present
importance of all the countries in Asia and Africa arises from the fact that
they are seeking by means of technical and industrial plant to become equal
partners with the countries of Europe and America. But Western civilization
excels because it is independent of both its Christian and humanist sources.
The development of technology and science in the West goes hand in hand
with a widespread secularization of human life and the disestablishment of
Christianity, hence Christianity to the Africans and Asiatics seems to be one
with a civilization which is already out of date, with a civilization which is
not one of work and technology' (p. 60).

[2] Our italics.

[3] *Op. cit.*, p. 419. See on this a remark by Jürgen Moltmann about the
Logos-concept of antiquity which still survives in Hazard's work: 'The
Greek term *logos* refers to a reality which is there, now and always, and is
given true expression in the word appropriate to it. In this sense there can be
no *logos* of the future, unless the future is the continuation or regular
recurrence of the present. If, however, the future were to bring something
startlingly new, we have nothing to say of that, and nothing meaningful can
be said of it either, for it is not in what is new and accidental, but only in
things of an abiding and regularly recurring character that there can be
log-ical truth' (J. Moltmann, *Theology of Hope*, London and New York 1967,
p. 17).

'*Finis saeculi novam rerum faciem aperuit*: In the closing years of the seventeenth century a new order of things began.'[1] However, Hazard has considerable difficulty in relating this 'newness' (*novam rerum faciem*) to the axiom that 'everything is in everything else' so that there is nothing that is new. 'We know this', he says. He *knows* that there is nothing that is new in the same way that the Christian *knows* that the Gospel is new. This knowledge is not scientific knowledge which can be deduced from facts of experience; it is a begging of the question and indeed an act of faith. Of course, everyone not only has the right to make acts of faith, he is compelled to make them. We must respect these acts of faith, while acknowledging that they are all different and cannot be reduced to a single position which would be more or less *natural* to every man. In any case there are two positions: there is the position of those who believe that there is nothing new, and there is the position of those who believe in the newness of the Gospel and who proclaim it to the ends of the earth. There is the position of those who regard the forward march of mankind as the segment of a circle which will ultimately come back to the same point and there is the position of those who believe that this march has a beginning and an end. Between these two positions a choice has to be made.

One may of course quote Ecclesiastes to show that the bible, in certain passages, has affinities with the pessimistic view of the world. This pessimistic view can be illustrated by the Greek myth of Sisyphus, doomed to never-ending beginnings, or the Hindu myth of Vishnu who brings our era (*Kali youga*) to a violent end by his tenth and final incarnation, *Klaki*, of which the symbols are the naked sword and the white horse, and this then leads to everything beginning over again. For Ecclesiastes, 'all is vanity' (1.2; 12.8). 'There is nothing new under the sun' (1.9). This seems very close to 'everything is in everything else; there is nothing that is new'. Yet if we examine his statements more carefully, we find that there are considerable differences. First, Ecclesiastes does not state that everything is in everything else. He believes in the living God whose action endures for ever

[1] *Op. cit.*, p. 420.

(3.14). Further, while he doubts if there is anything new under the sun, he is aware of the limits of his experience: 'I have seen the business that God has given to the sons of men to be busy with. He has made everything beautiful in its time; also he has put eternity into man's mind, yet so that he cannot find out what God has done from the beginning to the end' (3.10f.). God has vouchsafed to man the possibility of understanding the unfolding of the seasons, but unless God reveals it to him he cannot grasp whence nor whither time is going. This revelation reaches its culmination in the Gospel of Christ, which was unknown to Ecclesiastes. Nor was he a prophet, entrusted with proclaiming and preparing the way for the coming of Christ. He is essentially a seeker who believes; he is one who knows his limitations and for this very reason remains open to the divine possibilities. Indeed his message, taken as a whole, is not all discouraging. He is full of hope: 'Cast your bread upon the waters, for you will find it after many days' (11.1). 'In the morning sow your seed, and at evening withhold not your hand; for you do not know which will prosper, this or that, or whether both alike will be good' (11.6). The Bible of Jerusalem has this apposite note: 'These verses on risk allow us to appreciate the attitude which Qoheleth [Ecclesiastes] wishes to encourage in his disciple. He does not want to discourage him gratuitously, but to remove his illusions in order to spare him failure. In short, it is essential to take risks.'

The doctrine of evolution, which was an important corollary of the eighteenth-century scientific revolution, was fiercely attacked by traditional Christianity because its rigid determinism allowed one to conceive of nature apart from God. Today we are better able to appreciate those aspects of the theory of evolution that have been invested with a doctrinal character. That is why, despite grave dangers and errors, the masterly construction of Teilhard de Chardin[1] should receive our attention, for he has sought to harmonize the discoveries

---

[1] See G. Crespy, *De la science à la théologie. Essai sur Teilhard de Chardin*, Neuchâtel 1965. The author does not make sufficiently clear what is the principal danger in the concept of Teilhard.

relating to evolution and the biblical conception of the world. The discoveries relating to evolution, like the biblical message, give man a certainty that he is moving forward. For the science of evolution, as for the bible, there is no possibility of returning to our origins; the whole of creation is evolving in an irreversible movement. The greatness of Teilhard was to draw attention to the complexity of this movement and to set it free from both a mechanical determinism and an inevitable 'happy ending' for which there is no evidence. The Omega point, which is the term used by Teilhard to suggest the goal of evolution, will not necessarily be attained by progress in a linear direction. Teilhard has replaced the often simplistic idea of progress which derives from the nineteenth century with an idea of progress in which suffering is a necessary element. But this suffering, which is the product of imperfection and the straying aside of those beings who are the bearers of evolution, is not properly speaking a retreat. In any case the retreat is limited; it cannot be compared with the perpetual new beginnings found in the Greek and Hindu myths. It is the movement towards the goal that is the strongest. But this movement cannot be explained solely along rational lines. In Teilhard's view it includes the irrational under the form of mutations that cannot be anticipated.

The danger of Teilhard's concept lies less in his attempt to harmonize scientific and biblical evolution than in his idea of the relations between matter and spirit. He appears to have adopted a Hindu view which deprives matter of the reality ascribed to it in the bible by reducing it to a stage in the evolution towards spirit. Hence the whole of evolution becomes a fantastic history of the reduction of the material and of all the diversity it contains to a single point, the Omega point. Both Greek and Hindu wisdom are then right: everything is in everything else; there is nothing that is new. Teilhard's concept is identical with that of Aurobindo[1] which is inseparable from

[1] Aurobindo Ghose (1872–1950) was a Bengalee Brahman who, from the age of seven, was brought up in England. When he returned to India he began to study his country's religion, philosophy and culture of which he had

his yoga. It is true that the epistle to the Ephesians speaks of a
recapitulation of all things in Christ. It is sometimes suggested
that this is close to the Greek concept of gnosis, but the difference
is indeed very great. In the epistle to the Ephesians,[1] it is not a
question of a point but of an unimaginable fullness produced by
the *activity* of Christ or of God (1.23; 3.19).[2]

One of the characteristics of modern Western man is his
confusion with regard to evolution. At one time, he believes in
progress and is convinced that he is moving forward. At
another time, he is disillusioned and gives way to despair. One
day he is asserting his superiority, and another he is lamenting
his lack of usefulness.

It must be admitted that the Christian Church does not help
him very much to be freed from these alternatives. It does
believe in the forward march; it knows that it is the people of
God marching towards the City which God is making ready. It
believes, with the partisans of the doctrine of evolution, in the
irreversibility of the movement. It believes all this; but it
believes it *spiritually*, i.e. it does not include the world in its
belief. For it the world is only the necessary backcloth to the
drama of salvation. The classic example of this is provided by
Bunyan's *Pilgrim's Progress*. Hence there appear to be two
processes of evolution: the evolution of souls and the evolution
of the world. The first is that which is real, while the second is
relative and real only in appearance. Hence the Christian does
not share in the pessimism of 'everything is in everything; there
is nothing new', because he regards the Gospel as new indeed,
and his action in the world (other than the simple proclamation
of the Gospel and the welcoming of converts into the new
Noah's ark, the Church)[3] is characterized by a pessimistic

been entirely ignorant. For some years he was engaged in violent political
activity. He then withdrew from the world, with a circle of disciples, to
prepare the way for a mutation of humanity from the sphere of reason (mind)
to the sphere of super-reason, using a system of yoga which he called
'integral', since he tended to integrate matter and spirit in order to sublimate
the former. He founded an Ashram at Pondichery, near Madras.

[1] 1.10, 'to unite all things in him'.   [2] TWNT, VI, pp. 302f. (B3).

[3] *Cf.* J. Ellul, *Fausse présence au monde moderne*, Paris 1963.

relativism which is akin to that of the Platonist or the Hindu.

One of the consequences of this has been a reaction among Christians, and the 'Church and Society' Conference organized in 1966 by the World Council of Churches was an expression of this. The concern is now for the relation between the Gospel and the world. It has been realized that the Church should once again become the *avant-garde*, as in the apostolic age, instead of continuing to be as at present at the rear. Turned in on itself, it should open itself to the world. It should run the risk of living with its frontiers as ill-defined as those which now separate our country towns. All this is very right. The Church must rediscover its mobility. It must be open, for this is the will of its Master who is prepared to run the risks of this opening-up with it. It must incarnate itself. But as in every revolution – and this is indeed a revolution within the Church – the tendency is to radicalism. Hence there is talk not only of openness to the world but of conversion to the world.[1] It is stated that the distinctive mark of the Church is to have no distinctive mark.[2] An identification with the world, which is in fact a conforming to the world, is being preached. Any standing over against the world, any tension, is suppressed. God is indeed dead and the world is on its own, because the voice that should call to it is silent. There is no longer a word, for everything has become flesh. The incarnation does not culminate in the cross and resurrection but in absorption, in 'everything is in everything', which has been philosophy's last word from antiquity down to the present. If this is indeed what is wanted, would it not be better to admit that one does not know any longer what to do with the biblical concept of the world and so to adopt the Hindu outlook? But this is of course not what our revolutionary Christians want. Their reasoning takes its point of departure from the sovereignty of Christ, from the victory he has won and from his Kingdom that is coming. They are visionaries to whom the secularized

---

[1] H. J. Schulz, *op. cit.*
[2] 'The Church is pursuing a path of alienation. That it is unable to be recognized can be its distinctive mark' (*ibid.*, p. 102).

world of today is already the Kingdom *incognito*, and they mistake their hope for the reality. In this respect they go astray and lead others astray.[1]

In this situation the violent reaction of Jacques Ellul is quite understandable. 'The fact that Jesus Christ is indeed the Lord of the world does not in any way guarantee that the works which man does in this world express this Lordship, nor that they are entirely devoted to Salvation, nor that we can join in them unreservedly and without forethought. The world remains the world.'[2] In a later passage Ellul lists our confused ideas. 'Confusion between that History of which Christ is the Lord and the political or economic paths by which it is claimed that History may be accomplished; confusion between the Lordship of Jesus over History and the meaning of History as understood, for example, by a Marxist; confusion between the growth of the Kingdom of Heaven, of which the parables speak, and the progress of man in History; confusion between the goal of this History in the merciful hands of God and its culmination in a

---

[1] *Planning for Mission*, ed. T. Wieser, London 1966, p. 53. (This volume consists of selected papers written by the members of the North American and West European Working Groups on 'The Missionary Structure of the Congregation'. The French edition is entitled *Vers une église pour les autres*, Geneva 1966. The selection of papers is not identical in the French and English editions. Where the author quotes a passage that is in both I have reproduced the English version; where he quotes a passage which is in the French version alone I have translated accordingly. – Trs.) See also H. Cox, *The Secular City* – this latter expresses an exaggerated optimism. In his article on 'Mission in a World of Cities' (*International Review of Missions*, LV, 1966, p. 278), Cox is more balanced and reveals his awareness of the ambivalence of our present revolutions: 'The dangerous decades are the forty years in the wilderness and the urban revolution of our century in some ways duplicates the first deliverance from Egyptian colonialism. The same God who broke the shackles of slavery from the bodies of the Hebrews and led them by fire and cloud into a vocation in history is still calling men and nations. He still calls them out of death into life, out of slavish subservience into major servanthood, out of colonial dependence into responsible freedom, out of economic serfdom into self-reliance and adulthood. But between the call of God and the fulfilment of the promise there stretches the taut line of a danger. As a world of cities three billions of human beings have left the Egypt of the past and are headed for the promised land of the future. And we are all living in the dangerous decades.'

[2] See also J. Hammel in *Vers une église pour les autres*, p. 29.

technological or socialist paradise. . . . It is right and proper to rediscover that God reveals himself by means of a history and in History, but it is frightening to make this divine humility a motive, derived from pride, for the History of man.'[1] Here we are brought face to face with the *rigour, realism* and *wisdom* which Jacques Ellul said at the Conference on 'Church and Society' 'are also the gifts of the Holy Spirit' and of which Christians today must provide proofs within a pluralist and technological society.[2] Professor A. Rich of Zürich has also insisted upon the need for the Church to preserve the *tension* between the world and itself. 'Collaboration (*Partnerschaft*) in the form of precise relations between different persons or institutions only has meaning if it is between those who are unequal and who, while acknowledging that each has the same right, preserve a certain tension between them which corresponds to the values which they represent. True collaboration does not do away with this inequality nor with this tension; on the contrary, it affirms them.'[3]

We have now reached the heart of the problems which are presented to the Church by both its existence and its mission in the world. The sociologist Richard Behrendt sums up the position of the modern world very appositely: 'The world has been made dynamic by men of our kind (*unserer Art*, hence Western), as much in a positive manner by breaking innumerable ancient fetters and promoting a certain well-being as in a negative manner by promoting the dissolution of the organizations which provide security and protection and by creating international chaos.'[4]

It would be difficult to describe more succinctly the complexity and ambivalence of our world. All the gains achieved by those revolutions which shook the West and are now shaking the entire world have their opposites. Work understood as a ministry can become an idol; freedom from religious and other traditions can degenerate into anarchy; science set free from

---

[1] *Op. cit.*, p. 18.   [2] *Op. cit.*, pp. 21f.
[3] *Die Weltlichkeit des Glaubens. Diakonie im Horizont der Säkularisierung*, p. 85.
[4] *Soziale Strategie für Entwicklungsländer*, Frankfurt 1965, p. 54.

superstition can refuse any form of control and can throw the world into an abyss; respect for persons can lead to an a-social individualism; well-being can produce a collective egocentricity which leads men to arm themselves to the teeth in order to defend themselves against those who suffer deprivation. The revolutions from which we inherit what we have called 'acquisitions' are also responsible for unleashing a host of evil forces. These forces must be fought against. The Church, with its mission, has its place in the midst of this ambivalence.

Richard Behrendt, the sociologist, continues: 'This is why we (Westerners) should attempt to offer some possible solutions (*Ansätze*) and some suggested guide lines towards a new order which must be universal if it is an order at all.'[1] The Christian believes that this new order exists. It is the Kingdom of God which has drawn near in Jesus Christ.

Since then, this Kingdom has never ceased to draw near to men. It is this new and revolutionary order of God which gives them their *raison d'être* and their mission to those who accept it in faith and who are, in the world, its citizens and its heralds. To be a Christian is indeed to be a missionary within a revolutionary order.[2]

9 The Revolutionary Order of God

To be a Christian is to be a missionary within a revolutionary order. Within the context of the Third World this has especial point, because the Third World is at present living through what may be called the total revolution, in so far as it is trying to go through at one go a whole series of revolutions which in Europe took place over more than 1500 years. The nations of the Third World, involved in this revolution which they cannot avoid even if they would, need help from the West which is primarily responsible for this movement; this help must not

---

[1] *ibid.*, *loc. cit.* On the ambiguity of secularization see van den Heuvel, *op. cit.*, pp. 22–8.

[2] 'It is very difficult to be more revolutionary than the gospel is' (van den Heuvel, *op. cit.*, p. 39).

only take the form of equipment or economic programmes but above all of capable and devoted men who are ready to share the dangers of their situation with them. Further, Christians in the Third World are presenting us with the embarrassing question of the theological meaning of the revolutions in which they are involved. Those Western missionaries, both theologians and lay folk, who are already in this situation cannot wait for the Western theologians to publish their theology of revolution. They have had to formulate their theology often without knowing it well before the need was exposed so strongly by the Conference on 'Church and Society' at Geneva.

What is the role of a Christian in a revolutionary situation? In our view the reply to be given to this question is the specific missionary task of our generation. We can, however, make the question more precise: What is the *mission* of the Christian in a revolutionary situation? How can he be the herald and the witness of the revolution of God in Jesus Christ and of the new and truly revolutionary world which is coming into being?

In attempting to answer this question, we have first to consider two separate items. The first is the attempt to understand the world in which we live. This understanding must not be limited to a phenomenology of society. It is not enough to describe the revolutionary situations as they are nor to describe the phenomenon of secularization and of religious and social pluralism which are their corollaries. We have to go back to first causes and examine the history of the West. We have indeed attempted to sketch out the form that such research should take, but to be of help it needs to be carried out by a team of historians, sociologists and theologians.

The second item is the attempt to understand the particular meaning of the divine activity in Jesus Christ for the salvation of men as it is recorded in the bible. In what sense is the activity of God in Jesus Christ, with the reconciliation of men with God and of men with each other as its goal, truly revolutionary? What is the significance for our everyday life and for our activity in the world of the conviction that the fashion of this world is passing away, or, to put it another way, the recognition

of the relativity of all human effort and the obligation to perform this relative effort with a complete consecration within the
perspective of the world that is to come? Again, what is the
relation between man's activity, which is sometimes revolutionary, and God's activity, which is always revolutionary?
What place have prophecy, service and hope in this revolution?
When we have provided some answers to these preliminary
questions,[1] we can then go on to consider the most difficult
problem of all which presents itself to those Christians who are
aware of their mission to act as heralds and witnesses of the
activity of God in a revolutionary situation – that problem is
the one of the rules for action and of ethics. This ethic needs to
be both a norm and a situation ethic, i.e. an ethic which is not
simply the product of a situation but which brings the demands
of the Gospel into relation with the situation.

We are here touching on the very personal problem of the
Christian missionary.[2] Whenever a man succeeds in bringing the
demands of the Gospel into relation with the situation in which
he finds himself, this is a matter of pure grace; it is a sign of
the presence of the Kingdom and is a reason for thanksgiving.
Whenever success is not achieved, this is an occasion for
humiliation and suffering, with the assurance of forgiveness by
God, that his Kingdom may come through the acceptance of
humiliation and suffering.

In pursuing these two items, we shall have to touch upon a
very delicate subject. There are in the world forces opposed to
the revolution of God. But it would be quite wrong to assume
as some do that all the forces of the world are in opposition.[3]
We have to distinguish between the revolution of God, the
forces that are hostile to that revolution and those, like secularization, which, consciously or not, are in *sympathy* with it.

To be 'in sympathy' does not mean that these forces are to be
identified with the revolution of God, but that they assume a
similar or parallel direction. They are parallel because the men
who devote themselves to them, the majority of whom are not

[1] See Part II.   [2] See Part III.
[3] Such as Ellul, whose work has been quoted above.

Christians, are moved, consciously or unconsciously, by a faith which is parallel to Christian faith. This parallelism between certain revolutionary forces and the faith which moves them and the revolution of God, which is the subject and object of Christian faith, does allow, in our view, the possibility of an active Christian collaboration in all political and social projects which are striving to institutionalize certain aspects of the love of neighbour. The remarkable efforts in this field of sociologists and theologians should result in the formulation of some simple propositions which could be transmitted to the laity, for it is the laity who are today and will be even more tomorrow the heralds and witnesses of the revolution of God in Jesus Christ in a world in revolution.

The Mission of the Church

1 The Movement

'GOD *takes* us and *employs* us in his great movement of love which wishes to save all men.'[1] We shall understand nothing about the Church and its mission unless we examine them in terms of the great movement of God towards men.[2] The God of the bible is not a static God; he is not the philosophers' first principle from which all things proceed, but the living God who is untiringly concerned with his creation,[3] for it is his will that it should be free so that he may enter into a dynamic relationship with it, directed by a mutual love. God invites us to share with him in this remarkable undertaking.[4]

As we moved from Bali to New York, trying to find out what

---

[1] *Pain quotidien*, Lausanne, meditation of 29 July 1966 on I John 4.7–16.

[2] 'The triune God is the sole source of the missionary enterprise' (J. G. Davies, *Worship and Mission*, London and New York 1966, p. 30). In his chapter on 'The Meaning of Mission', the author shows how the Church is involved in God's mission and how the only conceivable form of the Church in its mission 'is that of a servant'. *Cf.* also: 'the church is only the church to the extent that she lets herself be used as a part of God's dealings with the oikumene. For this reason she can only be "ecumenical", i.e. oriented towards the oikumene – the whole world. Church-centric missionary thinking is bound to go astray, because it revolves around an illegitimate centre' (J. C. Hoekendijk, *The Church Inside Out*, London and Philadelphia 1964, p. 38; see further the whole section 'The Church in perspective', pp. 30–44). I am not sure that Hoekendijk has fully defined 'what exactly mission as contrasted to proselytism means' (p. 44). See my remarks on the views of Davies below (p. 95, note 2).

[3] John 3.16.

[4] In the Mission Centre in Basel there is a permanent exhibition, at the centre of which there is displayed the following definition of mission: 'The mission of God in Jesus Christ is directed to the world – it gives itself to it in service – it creates a new life.' To express this in a different way: it consists in a message and an act of service for the world, and these are offered with a definite end in view, viz. the renewal of life whereby the salvation of the world can alone be achieved.

the cities of Recife in Brazil, Calcutta in India, Hong Kong at the gates of China and Mexico in Latin America can tell us about the world in which we live, we discovered that the world is involved in an irreversible movement, the goal of which lies beyond the egotism of individuals who constantly seek to turn it aside; this goal is the quest not just for the well-being of a greater and greater number of people but for sufficient food for all.[1]

This irreversible movement is turning our world into a single world city;[2] its characteristics are ethnic and religious pluralism, the secularization of political and social structures and the transformation of human relationships and the methods of work.

This movement goes through periods of stagnation and periods of accelerated advance. The origins of the present acceleration are to be found in a remarkable series of revolutions. Faith discerns in these revolutions the fruits of prophetic preaching which involves man in the revolutionary movement of God; the goal of this movement is a dynamic and righteous order of living, firmly based upon a mutual love which will not fail because it is the outcome of free choice.

There is a correspondence between the movement we can discover in the world and the movement of the divine love which enfolds the world and humankind. This correspondence forces itself upon our attention despite the fact that for centuries the Church, adhering to a static conception of the world which it had inherited from antiquity, has constantly sought to keep it within narrow confines. As far as the discernment of this movement is concerned, the bible is up to date with the contemporary world, or rather the world is at last up to date with the bible!

This movement has burst into theological thought and is dominating present research.[3] A Church which is open to this

---

[1] *Cf.* C. H. Favrod, *La faim des loups*, Neuchâtel 1961, especially the chapter headed 'Le langage des chiffres', pp. 130ff.

[2] *Cf.* H. Cox, 'Mission in a World City', *International Review of Missions*, LV, 1966, pp. 273ff.

[3] 'It has been declared in ecumenical discussion that "There is no participation in Christ without participation in his mission to the world" (Willingen 1952). It is in God's own turning toward the world that the

movement can no longer rest content with the structures it has
inherited from 1500 years of static life; it must have new
structures.[1] Nevertheless, to examine everything in terms of
movement is to run the danger of neglecting its content.
Without content, this movement could soon end in an almighty
crash, like an aircraft without fuel, and would simply take its
place in the museum of human disillusion. Then the permanent,
the enduring, the static order, the *status quo* would again assume
their predominance as at the climax of the classical period,
which may be symbolized by gentlemen in periwigs. This
would mark the triumph of those who, with Ecclesiastes,
maintain that there is nothing new under the sun.[2] It is indeed
tragic that at the very moment when we are rediscovering the
mission of the Church and are busy trying to provide new and
dynamic structures so that it may fulfil that mission, a considerable number of theologians seem incapable of defining the
content of this mission. To the extreme radicals the Church is
indistinguishable from the process of secularization. Its message

Church is given its mission. Being caught up in that mission, the Church is
called to interpret the mighty acts of God in the world, both past and
present, and to celebrate them' (*Planning for Mission*, 1966, p. 222).

[1] This research underlies the material in *Vers une église pour les autres*, 1966.
This excellent collection of papers should be studied at the parish level, even
though there will be the danger of shocking people, as pastor Marc Boegner
says in his preface: 'But we must put up with the shock, for it is in itself a
summons to enter into ourselves, to think, to dig deep into the biblical
teaching, to pray. Above all let us not refuse to listen to those whose pessimism and desire to clear the ground may scandalize us; we are too ready to
listen to the optimists who do nothing to disturb us out of our continual
stagnation.' Albert H. van den Heuvel gives an impressive list of the
'renewal theologians', as he calls them: Wickham, Wentland, Visser 't
Hooft, Rahner, Küng, Kraemer, Weber, Congar, MacLeod, Gollwitzer,
Gibson Winter, Peter Berger, Hans Storck, Hoekendijk, Newbigin,
Margull, Abrecht, de Vries. After referring to them, he adds the witty
remark: 'When one goes through one's "renewal" library quickly, it seems
as if all these books are made up out of the same basic recipe – take a cup of
changed world, a teaspoonful of despair about the actual situation of the
church, and half a pound of request for total renewal' (*The Humiliation of
the Church*, 1966, p. 49).

[2] Ecclesiastes introduces into the biblical tradition some elements of
oriental pessimism which sees time as only an appearance and history as
an illusion, but Ecclesiastes is not without hope. (See above, pp. 44 f.)

consists of the proclamation of 'the freedom of Jesus for one's neighbour'; it is reduced to moral dimensions. The only 'irrational' element in all this is the idea of 'shock': the shock experienced by the disciples confronted by the resurrection, and the similar shock experienced by all those who are set free for their neighbour by the Gospel. This concept of 'shock' derives from a para-empirical form of thought which is acceptable to the most empirical of men.[1] This tendency to secularize the Christian message has been summed up in *Time Magazine*: 'The new approach to evangelism . . . is primarily interested not in selling Christianity but in sympathetically expressing human concern for others.'[2]

These observations require us to attempt to define the main lines of the Christian message in terms of the situation described in the first part of this study.

2 The Message

The *newness* of the good news proclaimed in the New Testament consists in the fact that the divine love, known to the men of the old covenant, has drawn near to all men in Jesus Christ and has given itself completely to them. Our generation is suspicious of love for two reasons. On the one hand, our literature, the cinema and sexual promiscuity have devalued its dynamic aspect, since they have been content to emphasize the sordid side and the possessive elements. On the other hand, bourgeois charity, which so easily becomes hypocritical, has undermined the idea of free gift. Hence there is more talk of service than of love and this indicates a passing over of the fact that service is an expression of love but cannot replace it.[3] Here we discover the dangerous modern tendency to confuse the container with the content, the expression with that which is to be expressed, and this is to believe that the moon is made of green cheese

[1] Paul van Buren, *The Secular Meaning of the Gospel*, London and New York 1964, pp. 148f.
[2] Atlantic edition, 14 May 1965, p. 42.
[3] See I Cor. 13.

(e.g. it is to identify secularization with the Kingdom of God). Now it is absolutely essential to preserve the tension between the container and the content; if we do not do this we cannot exercise our critical and prophetic role in regard to structures and we cannot continue to be an *'ecclesia semper reformanda'*, i.e. a church that is constantly reforming itself.[1]

The love which is directed towards another is a free gift. It is the basic element in the great divine movement to the world. Jesus tried to help us to understand this by his parable of the Prodigal Son. 'While he was yet at a distance, his father saw him and had compassion, and ran and embraced him and kissed him' (Luke 15.20). The Greek verb translated 'had compassion' belongs to those words which express most forcibly the feelings of a number of the characters found in the parables of Jesus.[2] It is in this way that Jesus describes the wholeness of the compassion by which God calls on man in order to save him.[3] The love of the Creator for his creature is then itself a movement, because it involves this extraordinary outgoing towards others which is beyond expectation and purifies, judges and regenerates. In our day there are few sermons about love. People are summoned to service, and there is good reason for this. But where is the fire that turns this service into an instrument of regeneration and of new life? To understand something about the mission of God in Jesus Christ and to become instruments of that mission, we must constantly return to Luke 15.20: 'while he was yet at a distance, his father saw him and had compassion, and ran and embraced him and kissed him'. Love is the essential content of the message addressed to men by God. This love involves three things which are of the utmost importance for us today.

[1] See also *de Oecumenismo*, II.6.

[2] The Unforgiving Servant, Matt. 18.23-35; the Prodigal Son, Luke 15.20; the Good Samaritan, Luke 10.29-37.

[3] 'The strongest expressions of human emotion are used to describe persons in the parables of Jesus, in order to signify the wholeness of compassion or anger with which God in his work of salvation makes demands on man.' TWNT, VIII, p. 554.

Creation

The divine love is expressed in *creation*. Empirically, we can do no more than recognize the existence of a world in evolution. But we have seen that the goal of this evolution is the object of an act of faith.[1] The same may be said of its origins. The bible invites us to make an act of faith, i.e. to acknowledge that this world has been *willed* by God, its Creator, in order that he may manifest his love within it. This world is therefore linked to the very life of God, to his dynamism and to his history. But this presence of God in the world does not mean that he identifies himself with the world. The bible reminds us constantly of the *distance* between the Creator and the creature. This distance, which is only discernible by faith, is also to be referred to history. Although the history of the world is linked with the history of God, the two are not the same.[2]

Creation culminates in man who is its centre. This is an affirmation of faith which supports certain evolutionary theories such as those of Teilhard de Chardin. When we speak of the world, of creation, and of the creature, we are referring to that created whole which is evolving and from which the human creature is detached at the point where, while still belonging to it, he is also distinct; as far as his spiritual and technological development are concerned, this assumes a considerable importance.[3]

The Covenant

The idea of creation is complementary to that of *covenant*. The bible is very explicit about this; indeed it has been said that it is its central theme.[4] It is because of the covenant that we can

[1] See above, pp. 42, 54.

[2] *Cf.* H. J. Schultz, 'History is God's exacting demand to keep pace with him' (*Conversion to the World*, 1967, p. 34).

[3] This distinction is also the object of an act of faith, which may support the idea of Teilhard of a continuity that bears within itself the possibility of a discontinuity (G. Crespy, *De la science à la théologie*, 1965, p. 42).

[4] See Gerhard von Rad, *Old Testament Theology*, I, E.T. Edinburgh and New York 1962, pp. 129ff.

grasp the idea of the distance between Creator and creature.[1]
What is the meaning of this covenant? It is not an agreement
between equals. The initiative always rests with God, who is the
only faithful partner in the covenant; it is he who ensures continuity amidst the unfaithful acts of his partner and it is he who
directs it towards its fulfilment in *communion*. We can only
appreciate its meaning with the help of the parable of father and
son. The relationship between Creator and creature which
ought logically to be modelled upon that of master and slave –
of the omnipotent master and the slave who is required to render
unconditional and blind obedience – is, through the willing love
of the Creator, modelled upon the relationship of a father and
his son; in this relationship, as soon as the son has attained
maturity, the obedience must be freely offered.

In our day there have been violent attacks upon the idea of
'person' and upon the parables related to it, especially on
grounds of paternalism. These images are said to derive from a
conception of the world that we have left behind. In repre-
senting God as a person seeking to enter into covenant with
other persons, account has not been taken of the development of
our thought and of our knowledge. Hence the substitution of the
concept of 'depth' for that of person.[2] We are of course in
sympathy with those who are struggling against the literal
interpretation of spatial expressions which, without question,
derives from a concept of the world which both Copernicus and
Einstein have overturned; these can only be used symbolically.
But if we have to be careful about speaking of 'in heaven', ought
we not also to take care in speaking about 'depth'? After all,
what is Paul Tillich suggesting when he speaks of a unity

---

[1] We prefer the concept of distance to that of discontinuity, because
what is important is neither continuity nor discontinuity, but the distinction
without which there can be no thought, no criticism, no reformation and no
redemption.

[2] 'To live serenely and courageously in these tensions (between negation
and affirmation of ontology) and to discover finally their ultimate unity in
the depth of our own souls and in the depth of the divine life is the task and
dignity of human thought' (Paul Tillich, *Biblical Religion and the Search for
Ultimate Reality*, Chicago 1955, p. 85).

between two 'depths', except a unity between our souls and the divine life? Since to express those things that demand an act of faith we have to use parables (depth is just as much a parable as is person), we do not see why we should not find them among the basic elements in human life. Hence there is no need for us to make any excuses for using the concept of person, which is after all very suitable for stating the message of a religion which understands God in terms of life and movement and not as a first principle.

The covenant, as we have said above, is the foundation of communion; it is the unchangeable and ever-repeated offer of the Creator to the human creature to enter into a relationship between free persons. The bible, in its account of history, begins with Abraham who has to leave his own country and his gods and become a stranger and a pilgrim so that he may join freely in the covenant to which he is called by God. His descendants, who are delivered from bondage in Egypt, vacillate continually between the flesh-pots of Egypt (i.e. the security provided by a static life linked to the soil and with gods that symbolize the ambiguity of nature) and the forward march, without any security, which is directed by a God who speaks. This God is a person, but he is not one who can be grasped; he is not one of whom an image can be made; he is not one who is satisfied with a ritual obedience which consists in the regular round of ceremonies; he demands the obedience of the heart from those who know that they will never have done enough.

An admirable summary of this history has been provided by Hosea:

When Israel was a child, I loved him, and out of Egypt I called my son. The more I called them, the more they went from me; they kept sacrificing to the Baals, and burning incense to idols. Yet it was I who taught Ephraim to walk, I took them up in my arms; but they did not know that I healed them. I led them with cords of compassion, with the bands of love, and I became to them as one who eases the yoke on their jaws, and I bent down to them and fed them. . . . My people are bent on turning away from me; so they are appointed to the yoke and none shall remove it. How can I give you up, O Ephraim! How can I hand you over, O Israel! . . . My heart recoils within me, my compassion grows warm and tender. I will not execute my fierce anger, I will not again destroy Ephraim; for I am God and not man, the Holy One in your midst, and I will not come to destroy (11.1-9).

Then comes the Son in whom the covenant is fulfilled. The instruction has been given; the cross, resurrection and Pentecost renew the covenant which henceforth bears the title of Gospel, good news, and this is addressed no longer to the descendants of Abraham alone, but to all mankind. 'For God so loved the world that he gave his only Son, that whoever believes in him should not perish but have eternal life' (John 3.16).

The Son's life among men, his death and resurrection, have laid bare the obstacle to man's response, with all his heart, soul and thought, to the divine offer: *sin, of which the fruit is death.*

Contemporary theology is in danger of minimizing the importance of this. Dominated by faith in the sovereignty of Christ over the whole world, it forgets that his victory has not yet borne its full fruit and that both sin and death continue to be realities which must be taken into account.[1] Love does not necessarily produce love; often it results in hate. There is in the depth of man a rebellious inclination which leads him to death. No one has succeeded in explaining adequately the source of this inclination. The story of the Fall relates it to the freedom given to the creature by the Creator and it is difficult to see that one can advance any further in understanding this mystery. Rebellion – sin – is the risk inherent in the freedom that has been given. Without this freedom there would be no father-son relationship but a master-slave relationship, as illustrated by the parable of the Prodigal Son (Luke 15.12, 21).

---

[1] 'The world – this secular realm – is the sphere of God's activity and Christ's Lordship. Within it, the Lord of the Kingdom is bringing his Kingdom's purposes to pass. But the realm of this world can never *contain* the Kingdom, though it should display it. And even the display or manifestation of the Kingdom within this temporal order is subject to distortion as well as incompleteness. Two great mysteries which are also undeniable facts contribute to this. They are the mysteries of sin and of death' (N. Goodall, *Christian Missions and Social Ferment*, London 1964, p. 111).

The Obedience of Faith

'Jesus Christ is the man who has truly fulfilled the office of man in a changing world; he is the firstborn among many brothers (Rom. 8.29), the second Adam (Rom. 5.12f.), the son of God obedient unto death on the cross; in whom God himself spoke, when in his dealings with man and the world he totally conformed to the will of God for man and the world.'[1] This fulfilment provides us with a third important aspect of the evangelistic message, that which concerns *method*. The rebellion that is an obstacle to the covenant is overcome by a particular form of service, by the *obedience of faith*, which involves self-giving. Chapter 13 of John is a perfect illustration of this. The service fulfilled by Jesus has two distinctive marks. By removing his garments Jesus shows that he is renouncing his status and is accepting the role of a slave, for in the ancient world semi-nakedness was a sign of a slave. The service that he renders springs from humility and indeed from humiliation. This act of service by the Son also bears a meaning which the service of a slave does not have – it purifies, it restores, it creates the circumstances necessary for communion signified by the meal that Jesus takes with his disciples. The Gospel of Mark summarizes the work of Christ in the world by saying: 'the Son of man also came not to be served but to serve, and to give his life as a ransom for many' (Mark 10.45). The present tendency is to stop at the words 'to serve' and to leave on one side the concluding words 'to give his life as a ransom for many'. Christ's service is not disinterested. He is concerned with nothing less than the obstacle which prevents the covenant offered by God to man from bearing fruit; he purifies and re-creates the conditions for a new life. 'Therefore if any one is in Christ, he is a new creation; the old has passed away, behold, the new has come' (II Cor. 5.17).[2]

---

[1] H. Schmidt, in *Planning for Mission*, p. 71.

[2] It is the time when the Church, through the spirit of the Son of Man, who was brought to the lowly state of a servant and exalted because of his perfect obedience (Phil. 2.5–11), will be led from truth to truth. See the

3 The Promise

Confronted with the forward march of the boys of Bali, we raised the question: where are they going? In the bible the city plays an important role: 'he has prepared for them a city' (Heb. 11.16). The Book of Revelation speaks of 'the new Jerusalem which comes down out of heaven' (3.12; 21.2, 10) in connexion with a *new heaven* and a *new earth* (21.1). These expressions are derived from Isaiah (65.17). In the parables of the Kingdom, Jesus uses images which describe fullness – the abundant fruit (the Sower); the wheat gathered into the barn (the Wheat and the Tares); the branches which provide shade for the birds of the air (the Mustard Seed); the risen dough (the Leaven); the treasure or the pearl for which one is ready to give up everything (the Hidden Treasure and the Pearl of Great Price); the fish collected in baskets (the Drag-net). His images of marriage or feasts describe a life of communion and joy. 'I came that they may have life, and have it abundantly' (John 10.10). All these

christological summary in Karl Barth's *Church Dogmatics*, IV 3, 2, translated by G. W. Bromiley, Edinburgh 1962, pp. 601 f.

In this context, questions arise about the beginnings of a Christian ethic. Jürgen Moltmann speaks of a 'public, bodily obedience' (*Theology of Hope*, 1967, p. 225 *et passim*), which is expressed in conflict with the godless world of the present. Beginning from the concept of fellowship (*koinonia*), Paul L. Lehmann has developed a style of ethics which is noteworthy not only because it has its starting-point in the community, but even more because it is orientated towards the kingdom of God and God's ultimate goal. Thus he can write: 'The dynamics and direction of God's activity are always toward bringing to light, from the foundation and centre of the "story" of his people, an actual foretaste of God's consummating purposes for them and for the world' (*Ethics in a Christian Context*, London and New York 1963, p. 70). Lehmann is really concerned with a 'messianic' ethic; for the 'politics of God', revealed in the Messiah, is both its basis and its aim. 'A *koinonia* ethic derives its theological foundation and focus from the way in which these doctrines define the meaning and direction of *the divine behaviour*, and thus also of *human behaviour*' (*op. cit.*, p. 105, my italics). See also p. 118: '. . . the full revolutionary bearing of the link between the messiahship and the mediatorship of Christ upon Christian thinking about ethics . . .'

See too: 'After Jesus Christ, history is directed towards a goal, it is dynamic history, like a seed which is cast on the ground (Mark 4), like the leaven which a woman conceals under three measures of meal (Matt. 13.33).' Paul Keller in *Planning for Mission*, p. 73.

concern the setting up of 'the great society of God', the foundation of which is the covenant; this covenant is offered freely by
the Creator to his creatures and when it is freely accepted the
result is a life which exceeds in terms of riches and harmony
anything that we could have imagined.[1]

This goal – this *telos* – of our forward march is difficult to
describe because it exceeds even our most advanced ideas, yet it
does not appear to be a problem to contemporary Christians
because they are more concerned with the movement towards
the goal than with the goal itself. There is no harm in this, as
long as we believe that we are not moving towards a restricted
life but towards its fullness. It is the vocation of the Christian
artist, by words, sounds, colours, rhythm and form, to help us to
feel this *fullness* of life.[2]

However, one of our present difficulties relates to the meaning
to be given to the verb 'to come', either when we pray: Your
Kingdom *come*, or when we speak of the Kingdom of Christ
which *is coming*. According to the parables of Jesus, it comes
incognito; hence it is already here; there is already a transformation in progress. But what meaning can we give it? What is
the relationship between this transformation which is due to the
leaven of the Kingdom, now in the dough of the world since the
coming of Christ and his surrender of his life on its behalf, and
the transformations which are taking place within the world of
which we have previously spoken? Paul Keller writes: 'Just as
this presence of Christ remains hidden, an object of faith not
sight, so the transformation of the world cannot be measured
nor its continuity laid bare. We even lack the words to talk
about it: whether we say progress, evolution, growth, maturation – all our words have overtones which make them suspect

[1] 'We have to manifest the adventurous faith that animated Abraham
when he left Ur of the Chaldees with no guarantee of security, with no
certainty about the future. Every Church which hears the call to preach
the Gospel reaches out to a goal which is other and greater than itself, with
its eyes fixed on the victory of Christ' (J. G. Davies, *Dialogue with the World*,
London 1967, p. 56).

[2] 'How can the least thing happen if the fullness of the future, if all time
complete, is not moving toward us?' So Rilke quoted by K. H. Miskotte in
When the Gods are Silent, 1967, p. 422.

and thus inappropriate. For we are dealing with a secret of which Jesus could only talk in parables: the world is living its history – which is positive – because of Jesus Christ.'[1]

We are in agreement: this does concern a secret. But this does not allow us to give up thinking about the value to be attributed to the words which 'have overtones which make them suspect' – progress, evolution, growth, maturation, development, etc., words which we frequently use because we are on the march. Do we believe as Christians that we can shape the future?[2]

Today or Tomorrow?

Christians may be divided into three groups according to their interpretation of Jesus' sayings about the nearness of the Kingdom of God. There are those who tend to identify political and social progress, achieved by science and technology, with the coming Kingdom of God. Christian faith then becomes an ideology fighting against other ideologies.[3]

At the opposite extreme there are Christians who regard everything that is done in the world as entirely valueless. 'There is no continuity between our history and the Kingdom, just as there is no continuity between our earthly life and our resurrection life. The "No" that God has pronounced over man, his works and his history, is a complete "No"; it is a radical and always present negative. . . . The bringing to nothing of the works of history is a real and complete overthrowing of them.'[4]

---

[1] In *Planning for Mission*, pp. 73f.

[2] According to the sociologist Behrendt, this belief is part of the third and final stage of a spiritual education for development. In the first stage, undeveloped man has to be led *to will* the development. In the second stage, he extends the horizon of his hopes; then comes the third stage when he himself takes part in the development because he believes it is possible (*Soziale Strategie für Entwicklungsländer*, 1965, pp. 174–9).

[3] 'Every time that this takes place, an ideology replaces faith. We forget that everything which is of this world is relative, and that "the fashion of this world passes away"' (I Cor. 7.31) – A. Rich, *Die Weltlichkeit des Glaubens* (1966, pp. 32f.). See also the remarks upon the relationship between personal faith and ideology in the article by A. Dumas, 'La fonction idéologique', *Eglise et Société*, Geneva, LV, 1966, especially pp. 41–6.

[4] Ellul, *Fausse présence au monde moderne*, 1963, pp. 22–5. This quotation only represents one aspect of his thought, but it is typical of a theology which

Neither of these two positions can be regarded as satisfactory. The first neglects the fact that the fashion of this world is passing away (I Cor. 7.31), while the second is unable to give any meaning to Christian action (apart from that of the evangelist or the Samaritan) and even less to the revolutions that have transformed our world and have set man free from false conceptions about work, religious tradition, the forces of nature, birth and well-being.

The Significance of the Provisional

In order to avoid either of these two extremes, we must seek to understand what Paul meant when he spoke of the fashion of this world passing away. That which is passing away – indeed that which must pass away unless we are to give way to despair – is everything that is marked by rebellion and death:[1] the fashion of the state, of society, of culture, of science, technology, economy and politics.[2] What remains is the direction given to man's action by the divine love and this expresses itself in a new attitude towards work (a co-worker with God), towards religion (worship in spirit and in truth), to nature (it is not sacralized), to people (there is no partiality, James 2.1, 9), and to well-being (there is a mutual sharing arising from love, I John 3.17). However, it must be emphasized that the *fashion* which even this new direction can assume in State, Church, society, culture, scientific formulae, technology of all kinds, economy and politics, *is passing away*. Further, it *must* pass away, because it belongs to the world that is marked with rebellion and death and cannot therefore give us satisfaction; it belongs to the

concerns itself little with the present transformation of the world. 'The great acts of God, creation and redemption, have taken place and, for 2,000 years, sacred history is, as it were, in suspension awaiting the final act. . . . Between the Ascension and the Parousia nothing real is taking place in the world; it is a period marked by an absence, by an emptiness which leaves a place only for an act of witness to the past event of the Son's incarnation and to the future event of his manifestation in glory' (Keller in *Planning for Mission*, p. 72).

[1] The *schemas* of this world, I Cor. 7.31.
[2] See Rich, *op. cit.*, p. 32.

provisional. But if this is the case, is it worth devoting our energies to forming this 'fashion'?

Our thirsty spirit is not easily satisfied with the provisional. Since the structures of the State, the Church, economy and all the others are provisional and destined to perish, it may seem useless to attempt to improve them or to change them. Both evolution and revolution appear to have little interest once their structures have passed away. But there does remain, as previously stated, the new direction of the individual within these structures. Hence we may conclude: let us concentrate on the attitude demanded by this new direction and let us leave the structures to themselves. If we were to do this, we would end up by endorsing the pessimistic viewpoint described above. Hence we must attempt to define our concepts more precisely, i.e. we must try to grasp the relationship between this new direction and the fashion that is passing away.

Faith and Para-faith

This relationship has been well described by Jacques Ellul. It is discernible by faith. 'That Jesus Christ is Lord from this moment means that there does exist from this very moment a new order within the disorder of the world, just as in each of us a new man has been born, although it would be presumptuous of us to think that this new man is to be identified simply with our present existence. Now no one belongs to this mysterious order, to this Kingdom of Heaven, as large as a mustard seed, hidden like a treasure in a field, except by an explicit act of adherence which is faith.'[1] This new order which exists from this moment within the disorder of the world is only discernible by faith and only the believer can have a part in it. With this argument we find ourselves in agreement up to this point, but to go further and assert that this faith must be explicit is to go further than Jesus himself (Matt. 7.21; 25.31–46). We have to acknowledge that it is possible to share in the new direction within the structures, that are destined to pass away and which are provisional, by means

[1] *Op. cit.*, p. 23.

of an 'implicit' faith, i.e. not articulated, imprecise and so a faith that is not 'a recognition by mouth and heart that Jesus is the Lord'.[1] This 'implicit' faith plays an important role in our secularized and pluralist society. Indeed it can be said that without it the several revolutions would have had no fruit, not even a provisional result, and would not be transforming the world in the way that they evidently are. In our world there is an immense number of men of goodwill whose concern for their neighbour springs undoubtedly from a form of faith, even if that faith is not explicit or is actually plainly false. The crypto-Christian humanism of the Renaissance has been taken up and developed by the Rights of man and by Marxism. A. Rich has shown that Marx, in his most acute insights, did see human nature as a complementary relationship finding its exemplary expression in the relationship between a man and his wife. This allows us to distinguish between a revolutionary attitude which is on the side of enslaved men and one which looks forward to the complete control by some men of all the others.[2]

The implicit faith of contemporary humanists is valid as far as the Christian is concerned in so far as it is a *para-faith*, i.e. a faith which manifests itself along lines parallel to those of Christian faith. This is not a question of any kind of faith. We have stressed, at the end of the first part of this study, that there is a considerable difference in structure between one faith and another, and we are not retracting this statement. We do not share in the new order of Jesus Christ 'by acting like everyone else and by fulfilling our professional and political functions',[3] but those who are moved by this faith which we have called para-faith *do not act like everyone else*. They are in fact distinguished from everyone else by their faith, and this distinction is quite evident. We soon know when a doctor is working for the welfare of those who are sick or if his profession is no more than

[1] Ellul, *op. cit.*, p. 24.

[2] A. Rich, 'Das Menschenverständnis beim jungen Marx und das Problem des Revolutionären' in *Glaube in politischer Entscheidung*, Zürich-Stuttgart 1966, pp. 80, 92.

[3] Ellul, *op. cit.*, pp. 23f.

a means of earning a livelihood—there are plenty of other examples.[1]

Para-faith is of value because it corresponds implicitly with certain important elements of Christian faith, such as concern for one's neighbour and hope for a better world order. *Nevertheless it is not faith.* Therein lies the missionary task of the Church: to call all those who are moved by a para-Christian faith – and these are to be encountered in all religions, and even among agnostics and atheists – to recognize it for what it is and then to take the step that makes it explicit, like Cornelius (Acts 10.34f.). Why is this? Because by its very nature para-faith is in a dangerous state of suspension and for this reason is more vulnerable than the faith that has openly found its basis in Christ: 'You are the Christ, the Son of the living God' (Matt. 16.16). Para-faith tends to attribute an absolute value to the provisional (e.g. the revolutionary achievements), and this can lead directly to ideological fanaticism; alternatively it may be swallowed up in scepticism.[2]

---

[1] *Cf. Conseils à l'intention des consultants internationaux*, United Nations, New York 1965; E. Heimann, *Du und die andern*, Berne 1965.

[2] See the remarks about P. Hazard at the close of Part One. F. Gogarten's remarks about secular man might also be borne in mind: 'The danger of fragmentation and the danger of new structures . . . these naturally threaten secular man to a particular degree. They demand his assertion of himself and his decision towards them in a way which was never possible in the case of mystical man, shut in on all sides by the world. For secular man, who has power over himself and is responsible for the world as his very own, is – in a word – historic man. But he can preserve his historicity only by being prepared at every turn for the fragmentation of the form he has won and the possibility of the emergence of new structures and, in this responsibility for what he does, by asserting himself over against anything that may appear on the horizon of the future, whether it is dark or bright. . . . He is thus always confronted with the temptation to approach all that is in questioning ignorance and to think of this as at his disposal' (*Verhängnis und Hoffnung der Neuzeit*, 1953, pp. 146f.). Here, of course, we must raise some questions. Does this hundred-per-cent secular man, who appears without any view of the world, any idea, any ideal, really exist? Since this 'truly secular' man can at best be an expedient for clarifying the ambivalence of secularity, we prefer to speak of men who can maintain their secularity because they have within themselves the unexpressed, unconscious faith which makes this secularity possible – a faith which we call 'para-faith'.

Making Use of the Provisional

It is by faith – explicit or implicit – that we participate in the new order which is within the world's disorder. Just as this faith partly transforms our inner being and this transformation is expressed in our outward action, so the participation of men and women in the new divine order expresses itself visibly in the world. Although this expression belongs to that which is provisional, it is nevertheless of considerable importance. It is a *sign* whereby we infer the reality of the new order within our disorder. Jesus laid special emphasis on these signs. It is true that the fashion of this world is passing away, but we must by faith make and remake this fashion in accordance with the new direction to which our life is devoted.

There is of course a great need for a comprehensive understanding of the value of the provisional. In the final pages of his monumental *Church Dogmatics*, Karl Barth has indeed provided one. He condemns in no uncertain terms those Christians who have no time for worldly realities and dismiss them as beyond hope on the grounds that their hope as Christians is in the last things.[1] The Christian has no right to be disinterested in penultimate things, according to Karl Barth, because he should know that 'in Christ's coming there will also be fulfilled all the expectations which he has had of him in his life in time if he is a good Christian. Again, in a way which is free and not rigid the Christian can and should, with the coming of judgment and redemption, turn from the goals in respect of which he has previously waited for him, since his awareness of the ultimate dénouement means that all the penultimate developments expected of him in time, while they are not destroyed, are set aside and stand in no further need of expectation.'[2]

The demons will exult, says Barth, if the sphere of the penul-

[1] He reminds them that 'the attempt is in fact an impossible one at its very root, and not merely in its consistent outworking. No one is able to concentrate so rigidly on the ultimate dénouement or to turn so resolutely from penultimate developments. The whole enterprise is a pious illusion' (*Church Dogmatics*, IV.3.2, p. 936).

[2] *Op. cit.*, p. 936.

timate is left empty through pure hope in the ultimate. Will there then be, before the coming of the Lord, a period of hopelessness through which the Christian will have to make his way, looking neither to right nor left? No, he says. If Christ is the goal and end of time, this means that time, with all its contents, is at least partly determined by the fact that it moves towards this as its end and goal.[1] With all men, the Christian is confronted with a world which appears to be abandoned to its own laws and in which nothing new seems to make itself manifest; moreover, for the Christian, this world is marked by sin and death. Yet he cannot shut his eyes to it nor seek refuge in the contemplation of heaven nor in waiting for the last day, because he sees in this world of the provisional or penultimate signs or indications of other things. 'What he expects in time is to come up against these indications, to perceive them as such, to be comforted and yet also startled by them, to be directed by them to the coming of the Lord, and to be prepared for it. *Just because the Christian hopes for the ultimate and definitive, he also hopes for the temporal and provisional.*'[2]

This hope for provisional or penultimate things in terms of the ultimate dénouement is genuine, according to Barth, when it fulfils three conditions.

It should not be bound to the changing conditions of this world, but should be affirmed even when the situation appears to be hopeless. One must hope against hope that the signs of the last things will be revealed.

In the second place, this hope must assume the form of an action corresponding to its concrete object. '*The Christian hopes as he serves*, and as he thus expects provisional and temporal encouragement, equipment and direction for his service.'[3] He

---

[1] *ibid.*, p. 937.

[2] *ibid.*, p. 938. My italics. *Cf.* 'For the ultimate meets us in the pre-ultimate, or temporal. And the Lord who comes towards us (and as such is our future) wants to visit us in those dark (or light?) years of 1976 or 1984. If we now prepare to go ahead, we see that, after all, something of what awaits us is already known: the world of tomorrow is already present. *Tomorrow is here.* The people of tomorrow have become our contemporaries' (Hoekendijk, *op. cit.*, pp. 170f.).

[3] *Op. cit.*, p. 938.

does not sit at the side of the road 'waiting for something to come and snatch him away, but will manfully go forward hoping for the concrete help needed to enable him to do so. In this respect, too, Christian existence is existence in movement. Hope takes place in the act of taking the next step. Hope is action, and as such it is genuine hope.'[1]

Finally, hope in the provisional in view of the ultimate is not a private matter but a public one. The Christian hopes 'in and with the community, and in and for the world. . . . For each new day and year the Christian hopes. He hopes that throughout the Christian world and the world at large there will always be relative restraints and restorations and reconstructions as indications of the ultimate new creation to which the whole of creation moves. And as he hopes for these indications, he knows that he has some responsibility for them.'[2]

These final paragraphs of Barth's *Church Dogmatics* are especially moving when compared with the first that he wrote. Extreme harshness has given way to a deep concern for man in his totality (*homo faber* and man as a social being), for all human activities destined to be provisional but whose provisional nature is one upon which God will pronounce not only his No but also his Yes. Hence in this respect Karl Barth is opposed to Jacques Ellul, who regards the No and the Yes of God as successive and not simultaneous, the No coming first and the Yes after it.[3] Of course it must be admitted that death comes before resurrection, but what Ellul appears to forget is that according to the witness of the Gospel – I nearly said the Gospel itself, i.e. the really good news – *resurrection begins before death*. This fact must be recognized, even though it is mysterious and hidden. But it is not without its signs, which may be discerned by faith and given their proper perspective. The Gospel of John provides the first systematization of this idea. Death is indeed death; it is real dissolution; resurrection is real resurrection; it is a real reconstitution. That is what Paul appears to be expressing by his images of the seed that dies, the clothing and the transfiguration (I Cor. 15.44; II Cor. 5.2; Phil. 3.21). But how can we assert

---

[1] *ibid.*, pp. 938f.   [2] *ibid.*, p. 939.   [3] Ellul, *op. cit.*, pp. 24–7.

that this dissolution and this reconstitution, over which Christ himself, under the divine sovereignty, presides, is achieved without any continuity?[1]

However, let us now discard these not very useful categories of continuity and discontinuity and concern ourselves instead with the *distinction* between penultimate and provisional things and the fulfilment of all things in Christ. At the same time, let us never forget that the fashion of this world is passing away (I Cor. 7.31) and that we are necessarily involved in the provisional by the form of service that God expects of us.[2] It is for Christ to draw out from us, from our institutions and our world those materials that can be used for the reconstruction of his Kingdom (I Cor. 3.12–15).

4 The Commission

It is to the Church that Christ gives the mission to proclaim and to live the message that we have just outlined. 'As the Father has sent me, even so send I you' (John 20.21). Over and above the disciples, this mission is given to all those who believe in Jesus Christ and constitute his Church. It is the whole Church as a body and consisting of individual members that is called to bear witness to the message of the Creator's love for his creation. Recent studies have recalled us to this truth and we do not need to enlarge upon it.[3] But there are three problems to which we

[1] 'There is no continuity between our history and the Kingdom, just as there is no continuity between our earthly life and our resurrection life' (*ibid.*, p. 22).

[2] Paul Lehmann's remarks are interesting in this context: 'The Christian interpretation of behaviour starts with and stays within the context of the fact of the new humanity. In this context behaviour is, if anything, more dynamic, more on the move, and more informal than the pattern of movement from the partial to the perfect can accommodate. The fact of the new humanity . . . means that all behaviour is a fragmentary foretaste of the fulfilment which is already on its way . . . "Power and glory" denote the final and radical transvaluation of the whole created and historical order of which the second Adam and the new humanity are a guarantee and foretaste' (*op. cit.*, p. 122. See also p. 65 above).

[3] *Cf. Ecclesia peregrinans natura sua missionaria est, cum ipsa ex missione Filii missioneque Spiritus Sancti originem ducat secundum Propositum Dei Patri.* Vatican II, Decree on the missionary activity of the Church 2.

must direct our attention. The first relates to the form of this witness, the second to its motives and the third to the organs by which it is carried out.

(a)   *Witness through Presence*

It is the current fashion to speak about *presence*. When '*presence in the world*' has been said, it seems that everything has been said. Our criticisms of Jacques Ellul should not be taken to mean that we do not appreciate the importance of his warning: 'False presence in the modern world'. There is a kind of presence which is not really a presence because faith can no longer perceive it. Out of a fear of spiritual pride and a concern for solidarity, the salt can lose its savour; the lamp is hidden; in short, we just resign ourselves. There is nothing surprising in resignation; Jesus himself accepted it and we should perhaps be more resigned than we often are. It is of course wrong to be utterly given up to resignation, but is it not worse to pretend that this particular form of resignation is the new mission to which the Church is being summoned? We should indeed be very careful in speaking about the presence of the Church in the world. We can make the point more clearly by referring to a recent definition of the Church. 'The Church is nothing other than *a segment of the world* which confesses the universal Lordship of Christ: thus it is the place where the world becomes aware of its true destination, its true face.'[1] The expression 'the Church a segment of the world' would be acceptable if, for its author, this 'segment' were indeed the *place* where the world becomes aware of its true destination – the place where the world is *converted*. But his later remarks render such an explanation difficult. 'At no time may the Church separate itself from the world by placing itself in the impossible position of spiritual pride.'[2] We agree that the Church should not separate *itself* nor put *itself* at a distance from the world through spiritual pride, but if this means that the Church is not 'separated' nor 'distant' from other parts of the world, then we have to sound a warning. We do believe that the Church is that *segment of the world*, that *piece of the world* – to use

[1] G. Casalis in *Planning for Mission*, p. 123.   [2] *ibid.*, *loc. cit.*

George Casalis' words – which has been chosen by God in Christ by pure grace to be the witness of his message of love. The grace and the vocation of which it is the object create a distinction between this piece and the others and this distinction is the essential condition for its act of witness. It must be admitted that both the vocation and the grace which make the Church a part of the world distinct from other parts can become the grounds for spiritual pride. The entire history of Israel and of the Church reminds us of this fact. This pride is a sign that the Church, despite its election, is not only in the world but of the world and that it can fail to understand its vocation, refuse grace and live autonomously, i.e. falsely separated from God and the world. This pride has to be fought against. But if we wish to prevent it by not allowing the Church to be the Church, i.e. to be that 'segment of the world' that God sanctifies by his presence, we are perpetrating a misunderstanding.[1]

In the light of what has been said so far, we can say that *presence* is indeed the constitutive form of the Church's mission in the world.[2] Mission also assumes other forms, but they are derivative from that of presence. It is always by its presence that the Church fulfils its mission. The imperative 'go' which Jesus uses so often implies a movement, a change of place, the crossing of some frontier or other and so makes us aware of the dynamic structure of this presence. Moreover, when Jesus sends his disciples to the ends of the earth to 'make disciples of all

[1] 'The truth that Christ the Lord wills to be proclaimed in every way and that he sovereignly makes use of even the sinner does not mean that the Church will not and should not be the first place in which the Lord finds obedience and thus the realization of his will. If Jesus Christ makes history as the Word incarnate, then it is not his will to reach the world despite of and without the Church. The Church itself is part of the world that he means to make obedient to his will. . . . The community is therefore first a part of creation, which is encountered by the word of the Lord; it is thus primarily part of reality, of the "public", to which the Lord's word applies' (H. R. Müller-Schwefe, *Die Lehre von der Verkündigung. Das wort und die Wirklichkeit*, Hamburg 1965, pp. 85f.).

[2] 'The basic form of witness is presence. . . . To exist in a situation with a sense of responsibility towards men in it, and with the constant intention of witness to the Christ-event within it, this is the essential form of mission' (R. K. Orchard, *Missions in a Time of Testing*, London 1964, p. 92).

nations ... baptizing them ... and teaching them to observe all
that I have commanded you' (Matt. 28.19f.) it is so that they
may be amongst these nations what they are by grace: the salt
of the earth, the light of the world, the leaven in the dough,
because apart from this form of being, this presence, their
witness by word of mouth cannot 'make disciples'.

Recent studies have emphasized that the mission of the people
of God in the Old and New Testaments is accomplished by an
outward movement, i.e. by their presence.[1] Without denying
the scriptural basis of the traditional concept of mission, viz.
that it is an undertaking to win mankind to faith, Martin-
Achard has emphasized that 'the result of its centrifugal movement is a great regrouping of mankind . . . in the presence of
Christ'. It is by his action within the Church that Christ converts
the nations. Hence 'the Church does its work of evangelization
in the measure in which its Lord gives it life; when it lives by
him its very existence is effectual. . . . Mission . . . is entirely
dependent upon the hidden activity of God within his Church,
and it is the fruit of a life really rooted in God. The evangelization of the world is not primarily a matter of words or deeds: it
is a matter of presence – the presence of the People of God in the
midst of mankind and the presence of God in the midst of his
People. And it is surely not in vain that the Old Testament
reminds the Church of this truth.'[2]

We must examine this presence very carefully. It concerns not
any kind of presence but a *missionary* presence. It is missionary
first of all because it is the instrument of the *missionary presence of
God* in the world. This particular presence assumes the form of a
visitation. In Jesus Christ, God visits men (Luke 1.78f.). He
unites himself with their life; he shares in their joy and their
suffering, but he is always a *visitor*, one who cannot be forced
into line nor imprisoned within the established order; he is one
of whom one rids oneself by nailing him to the cross.

The missionary presence of God in the world has three

[1] R. Allen, *The Spontaneous Expansion of the Church*, 2nd ed., London 1949;
J. Blauw, *Gottes Werk in dieser Welt*, Munich 1961.
[2] R. Martin-Achard, *A Light to the Nations*, E.T. Edinburgh 1962, pp. 78f.

important aspects. The presence of Christ in the world is a dynamic presence, directed towards a goal. The visitor is present on behalf of those whom he is visiting, in such a way that his presence is always directed towards them, always on the watch, wide open to all possibilities and at every moment ready for service. The presence of the visitor of God, Jesus Christ, is then service and presence *on behalf of*.

While ordinary visitors leave as they came, the visit of God to men in the person of his Son is entirely different. Christ does not leave as he came. He gives himself, body and soul, for the men and women of Galilee, and Judea and for his disciples. When he has reached the full extent of his love by accepting the full extent of his humiliation, then he is liquidated, he is killed. His visit runs up against a complete lack of comprehension. God makes this lack of comprehension, which has been accepted and borne for the salvation of men, the instrument of their salvation.

Finally, Christ's visit also has about it a certain degree of *distance*. Despite the incarnation and the solidarity in the sufferings, service and offering of his life, there is between Christ and those whom he visits a disturbing distance. He remains the visitor. He is constantly to be distinguished from others. He is not simply assimilated with those who surround him, although he does share their life and accepts their conditions without restriction.

Dynamism, ultimacy and distance are the three characteristics of a truly missionary presence and they are to be discerned in those whom Christ sends to the ends of the earth to be witnesses of his words and deeds, as well as of his coming, his service, his death and his resurrection. Their presence is essentially active because it is determined by mission and is directed towards others with a precise goal, i.e. the salvation of all creatures and all creation. The Church as a body is not just simply present in the world. It is only present to the extent to which it is directed towards men and is really a Church for others. Its physical presence is not in itself missionary. It is possible to remain for years in a family, a factory or an office and still be turned in on oneself. Missionary presence involves a movement towards others. Most of the time, this movement is independent of physical circumstances; it derives from the most active centre within a person, because it is a movement from the heart for which the Spirit is responsible.

The Crossing of Frontiers

Although in the majority of cases this movement takes place within the immediate neighbourhood, in others it involves the crossing of frontiers which are geographical, cultural, linguistic, national and racial, because it is always possible that where we are physically is not where the Spirit wishes us to be. Mission has for too long been regarded solely as the crossing of geographical frontiers; whereas we are now aware that mission does not necessarily involve a change of place. There is a mission to be fulfilled near at hand as well as at a distance. Nevertheless, missionaries are not always on a journey; at the end of their travelling, they are required to fulfil their mission where they are by their presence. It is their presence in the country to which they have come which is missionary and not their setting off nor their journey. With good reason there has been opposition to the romanticism connected with leaving one's country behind, because this has turned attention away from the missionary reality. The changes taking place in our world are removing the 'romance' from mission, because today everyone is on the move and everyone is going to another country. There is nothing extraordinary in going from one continent to another, from one climate to another or from one culture to another. An increasing number of Christian and 'neutral' organizations are sending volunteers and experts into distant countries just like the missionary societies.

In a world where exchange of personnel is ever increasing, it may seem that mission, in its traditional form of crossing frontiers, will continue. But this is not so, for the existence of Christian Churches in all continents is leading many to think that the sending of missionaries is unnecessary. The handicaps of going to another country are then listed – the difficulties of language, of an imperfect knowledge of the situation, of being a foreigner, of belonging to a people or a race which has lost its popularity in the world at large – and the conclusion is drawn that the ministry of the native, whether he be a man of Zürich, a Nigerian or an Indian, is preferable to that of a foreigner. But this reasoning is false.

In the first place, it derives from a static conception of the world and does not take account of the immense changes that have occurred over the past 150 years. Further, it suggests that the Church is an association of 'national' Churches or *Landes-kirchen*, each with its own life and quite satisfied to acquiesce in peaceful co-existence. Finally, this form of reasoning does not take account of the power of the Spirit who does not bother about the frontiers which the Churches have created between themselves and who continues to blow where he pleases and to lead an ever-growing number of men and women from their countries to others so that they may be, as strangers and visitors, the witnesses of the fullness of the life of the Church spread throughout the whole world.

More than ever, a Visitor

Since those Churches, which were the outcome of mission, have become autonomous, many things have changed. The foreign missionary has become without any question a *visitor*. It is true to say that mission has always had this aspect of a missionary visit rather than of a spiritual colonization, but in present conditions this aspect has been emphasized. Most missionaries today have the status of visitors, which often restricts them, because they are coming to a task which is the prime respon- sibility of the Christians who live there. The tact required of visitors is required in even greater degree by those visitors sent in the name of Christ, the visitor of God. We are not talking about a visit out of politeness or friendship; we are referring to a *missionary visit*, the aim of which is to include the visitor in the mission which is laid upon the Church he is visiting. This is the aim of the visit that Paul was going to make to Rome (Rom. 1.8–15; 15.14–21). These verses reveal the immense tact and respect for liberty but also the absolute firmness of intention with which Paul made preparations for his visit to Rome.[1]

Christ has opened the way of service for his disciples. We have not to open it again, but we have to march along it. It is a way of humiliation, for the hostility which brought Jesus to the cross is still manifested towards his followers. The visitor soon finds out that he is not being treated with the honours due to a visitor but as a despised foreigner or as the least of servants. His presence, which is directed towards the well-being of those amongst whom he has come, full of the joyful Yes of the Gospel, is then transformed into humiliation and suffering. But it is only by accepting the unjust acts of humiliation and by taking upon himself the undeserved suffering that the servant-visitor becomes the instrument of the visit of God, and is truly salt, light and yeast. It is in this way that he becomes supremely active, although he may appear to be passive; it is in this way that his presence in the world is truly missionary.

There is also for the disciple, fulfilling the role of a visitor, as there was for his master, this disturbing element of distance. There is a limit beyond which he cannot identify himself with another if he wishes to continue to be a messenger and a witness. In order to be a man for others, he must live with Christ. We are not of course talking about a distance created by our standard of life or by some imagined superiority; we ought always to allow ourselves to be liberated from that distance by Christ. We are, however, talking about that distance which Christ alone has bridged by his death and resurrection, of that distance which ceases to exist only in faith and in the communion which recalls the Lord's death and proclaims his coming. The bible constantly asserts that those who share in the mission of God in this world are strangers. The classic passage is verse 13 of Hebrews 11: 'strangers and exiles on the earth'. As long as we remain in our own neighbourhoods, the meaning of this is scarcely appreciated.

[1] See Acts 15.36 and the article on *episkeptomai* in TWNT, II, pp. 595–602. Re *episkeptomai* R. A. Lambourne says: 'There is a considerable difference between this type of visit, and one which is a purely private act of good work done by an individual humanitarian' (*Community, Church and Healing*, London 1963, p. 115).

We have to cross frontiers of language, culture or race to understand fully what 'being a stranger' is – it is never being able to identify oneself wholly with another and so being always a visitor. This involves suffering for those whom one visits as well, because they are brought into collision with this distance which cannot be done away with apart from faith and communion. But God uses this reciprocal suffering to keep us on the watch and to further his work. This was recognized by the missionary conference in Mexico: 'in the providence of God the very handicaps and frustrations of foreigners may be for the furtherance of the Gospel and part of the wisdom of God (I Cor. 2.7)'.[1] It was to a man whom he had first made a stranger that God confided his first mission – to Abraham. As a stranger, he was able to achieve things which a native would have found impossible. But God works with both; he entrusts his mission to a native and to a stranger. We should make use of the missionary resources represented by the many strangers in the places where they are now living; we are greatly lacking in imagination in this respect. The studies on the missionary structure of the congregation disregard these possibilities, except in so far as they envisage the role of the laity.[2] No doubt this arises from their refusal to accord any importance to geographical, cultural, linguistic, racial and political frontiers in a world that has become one. This is a serious mistake. The unity of the world and the Church can only develop if there is an increase of ministers equipped to cross frontiers and capable of taking upon themselves the tensions which such a crossing involves.

Conversion and Communion

The efficaciousness of a dynamic Christian presence in the service of others, which is aware of the distance which faith in Christ imposes upon it in relation to the world and to those who do not share this faith, rests upon two factors: conversion to God and communion with him in Christ.

In order to fulfil his mission, simple presence in the world is not sufficient for the Christian; he must be in communion with

[1] Section 4, 4f. of the Report.   [2] *Planning for Mission*, p. 170.

his Creator and hence he must accept the No which the Creator pronounces upon his heart, his thoughts and his works, while at the same time he turns with confidence to the Yes of grace which creates all things new. In other words, he must be converted and must continue converted and be oriented towards his Creator. At the present time, this primary condition for a truly missionary presence (any other presence is that of everyone else and hence is useless) is being neglected. It is as if goodwill and the willingness to serve can replace conversion. It is of course true that conversion is a term that our contemporaries do not like, yet this is a mistake, for it would be difficult to find a more dynamic one.[1] Conversion involves a converging movement in a quite definite direction; it is therefore fortunate that an attempt is being made to rediscover its meaning.[2]

Conversion opens the way for that communion to which we are being called by God. Communion does not do away with the distance that separates the Creator from his creature, but it does provide the starting-point for a new relationship and for a continual exchange which generates life, joy and power. Com-

[1] 'Indeed I would be glad if the term conversion could be dropped from the Christian vocabulary; its continued use misleads many as to the challenge of the Gospel. . . . I do not wish to deny that men are called to acknowledge the Lordship of Christ, but this involves *metanoia*, i.e. repentance, which refers to a change of direction and not of place, to the acceptance of obedience to God's will in the world and not a movement out of it into a religious society' (J. G. Davies, *Dialogue with the World*, p. 54). I do not quite understand the distinction between a change of direction and a change of place. A change of direction involves a person in a movement and this movement may well require of him a change of place, as in the case of Abraham. Albert H. van den Heuvel gives the following definition of the term: 'Conversion that precedes, produces, and sustains renewal means the rediscovery of the nature of God's calling to be a servant community to the world. *Metanoia* can only be a recognition of our place in God's work in his world' (*op. cit.*, p. 154).

[2] The term is the object of a study promoted by the Division of Mission and Evangelism of the World Council of Churches. A first step has been embodied in a document entitled 'Conversion to God and Men. A Study Document on the Biblical Concept of Conversion' (WCC, DWME, 60–90, London). Paul Loeffler, the author, ends with a quotation from Bishop Newbigin: 'Conversion is a turning round in order to participate by faith in a new reality which is the true future of the whole creation' (*International Review of Missions*, LIV, 1965, p. 149).

munion is based upon participation. At the present time this is focused in the eucharist where Christ offers himself to the faithful in the bread and the wine and where the faithful in their turn offer themselves to Christ (Rom. 12.1–3) by accepting the signs of participation.[1]

In order to be salt, light and yeast, we must participate in the life of him who is the true salt, the true light and the true yeast.

Worship[2]

Communion, which is the fruit of conversion, is the necessary condition of an effective presence in the world. It concerns each Christian individually and all Christians corporately.[3] It is by

[1] 'Authentic worship is therefore that in which the two dimensions are combined, viz. participation in Christ through communion and so participation in his mission to the world of man' (J. G. Davies, *Worship and Mission*, p. 98). Later Davies writes: 'Once we take historical existence seriously, then we have to pay attention to all three points of the eucharistic reference. It is the immediate future in the world that becomes our concern, and the cultus must be open to that future, because open to the consummation, and so enable us to be co-workers with God in its creation' (p. 108); see the whole section on 'The Meaning of the Eucharist in terms of Mission', pp. 92–112.

For Hoekendijk 'communion must as a matter of course be an *eschatological order*: that is to say, open-ended and so structured that we can have this order "as if we did not have it"' (*op. cit.*, p. 164). Here is his challenging definition of communion: 'Communion as an eschatological Sacrament is the representation of the Kingdom in the *world*; it is impossible to lock up the Kingdom in the church, and it is equally impossible to make this Sacrament of the Kingdom a purely churchly event. Finally, Intercommunion is not a question between denominations but between nations; not of Intercommunion between all sorts of confessions but between people of all sorts. Communion is the first fulfilment ("The new order has already begun!") of the "feast that the Lord will make for all nations" (Isa. 25.6). So plans and practices of Intercommunion will have to be extended to the "many [=all nations?] for whom the blood of the covenant was already shed" (Matt. 26.28)' (*ibid.*, p. 163).

[2] The author regrets that J. G. Davies, *Worship and Mission*, was not known to him when he wrote this section and urges the reader to consult Davies' book for a full treatment of the subject. Davies' main thesis is that 'worship and mission are not to be conceived as two distinct activities, the one theocentric and the other anthropocentric; both are aspects of a single divine activity in which, through Christ, we are included' (p. 71, see also p. 92).

[3] 'The koinonia is the place where the shalom is already lived. As such, the Christian community belongs to the new age. That means that this

his private devotions as well as by his joining in corporate worship that the Christian is trained to be what he is by the will of Christ: salt, light and yeast.[1]

In connexion with personal devotion and common worship, both essential for the missionary presence of the Church in the world, there are two things to be said. Some Christians rest all their hopes on liturgical renewal, while others consider that public worship is no longer relevant to our secularized and pluralist society. This contradiction is perplexing and we need to examine it with care. Emphasis upon the liturgy is valid in so far as the term 'liturgy' is given its primary meaning of service in which the whole community shares. The primary aim of liturgy should be so to arrange the acts of worship that their intention is quite evident and the community is enabled to play a full part in them. The best type of liturgy is one which has a simple and clear order with scope for variety. There is nothing more tiring for a community than to be faced with either never-ending improvisations or constant repetition. The great danger in the present Liturgical Movement is the threat of succumbing to an aesthetic outlook based upon archaeology and history. By

---

fellowship of the partakers of the same salvation is nothing more in this world than a company of strangers and pilgrims (I Peter 2.11), a paroikia, or group of sojourners in the world, fully detached and therefore free to relate itself to every form of existence. The Christian community, therefore, is (or should be) an open community, open to everyone who has become a partaker of the same shalom' (Hoekendijk, *op. cit.*, p. 27).

[1] During the Conference on 'Church and Society', *La Vie Protestante* of Geneva asked E. C. Blake, the secretary general designate of the World Council of Churches, how the Church could contribute to the transformation of society. He replied: 'Above all by its regular acts of worship offered to God. According to our several traditions we read the bible; we pray, we give thanks, we make petitions and we intercede; we administer the sacraments; and we sing to the glory of God. In the majority of our Churches there is preaching and biblical instruction, and the preaching concerns the specific problems of the congregation, both as individuals and as a community. I am taking this opportunity to refer to this because certain of us, in our great desire to improve upon the past, forget the central importance for the Church of the offering of worship to God. Unless I believed this I would long ago have joined my efforts to some other institution which may be more effective in achieving social change' (*La Vie Protestante*, No. 28, édition vaudoise, 5 August 1966, pp. 3, 5).

going back to the sources, we end up with services which can only move those who know the writings of the patristic era and the ancient basilicas. Tradition has no value unless it has been itself inspired by a sense of mission and is able to assist the missionary presence of the Church at the present day. We must at all costs avoid the possibility that our participation in public worship should require a liturgical and musical knowledge which is beyond most people. We need to remind ourselves of Paul's admonition to the Corinthians about speaking in tongues: 'If, therefore, the whole church assembles and all speak in tongues, and outsiders or unbelievers enter, will they not say that you are mad?' (I Cor. 14.23). There is good reason to think that there are many who no longer take part in public worship because they are no longer among the 'initiated'. If we want the Sunday worship to be public and therefore missionary, we must see that its form does not create a useless distance between the Church and the people around it, whether this be in Lausanne, Basel, Accra or Djkarta.[1]

Failure to adapt forms of worship to present circumstances has led some Christians to reject tradition and to make innovations at all costs. For more than thirty years all kinds of experiments have been going on in all parts of the world in an attempt to adapt worship to the surrounding popular culture. These efforts are to be welcomed, if only because they represent a real struggle against the sterility of traditions which have been taken over by generation after generation without any critical examination.[2] Yet the results of these attempts are not always encouraging. The reason for this is a failure to appreciate the real

[1] For the role of outsiders in worship see *Planning for Mission*, pp. 190f.

[2] 'If we want to worship in our day of creative doubt, we shall have to discover that the heart of our society beats in its experiments. Experimentally, we can come to an authentic expression of the Christian faith in an industrial and scientific society. If only the hymnologists would understand what they do to people by forcing them to sing out their faith in terms of nature! Look at our psalms and hymns! Not a word about cars, bridges, housing projects, motor ways or power plants. In the worship of the Christian church, modern civilization stands implicitly judged: it is not good enough to provide the metaphors of the liturgical language' (van den Heuvel, *op. cit.*, p. 83. See the section on 'Worship in a Secularized World', pp. 77–91).

problems of the renewal of worship and its adaptation to the surrounding culture. Christian worship is an actualization of the
covenant that the Creator offers to his creature, and for this very
reason it is different in its basic structure from all other forms of
worship in the world.[1] This question of structure is too easily
neglected in favour of a consideration of the separate elements
in worship[2] – prayers, songs, recitals, sacramental acts, all of
which are present in other forms of worship. It is of course
possible to take the attitudes, tunes and customs of a local form
of worship and integrate them with Christian worship. But it
must not be forgotten that when this happens these elements are
transformed.[3] For example, we can take over a fine Hindu
melody which has been used to call upon the name of a god and
adapt it for a psalm or Christian hymn; but from the moment
that such a melody, originally devised for an act of individual
piety, is taken over by a community, it is transformed; it ceases

[1] van den Heuvel draws our attention to the relation between worship
and our ethical situation: 'All experts have pleaded for strong and con-
vincing and factual counteraction against the despair that our absurd
situation produces. Of course we all agree with that request. But fundamentally that demands a living out of hope and certitude that we hardly
know any longer. It needs more than an intellectual approach to the matter;
it also needs more than a grim counteraction in politics. The Christian
community has little else to offer the world here than the very heart of her
belief: the hope that is exactly through absurdities – "foolishness" as the
Bible says (I Cor. chs. 1 and 2) – that God saves his people. The way in
which we express this is our worship. The great liturgical traditions are
better equipped here than the Protestants. If worship is nothing but an
order of service, there is little strength against the power of despair and the
absurd. I do not think we can do with less than something like the liturgy of
Chrysostom with its power. . . . The Revelation to John is the Liturgy of the
Absurd that needs further working out. In the light of our ethical predica-
ment, the liturgical movement needs to renew both the dramatic and the
simple elements that have always accompanied the people of God' (*op. cit.*,
pp. 154f.).

[2] 'The primary factor therefore in determining the order of service is
whether or not it is a means of communicating the *kerygma* and is relevant
here and now in this context. Participation in the *missio Dei* puts repeatedly
to all liturgical forms the question: why?' (Davies, *Worship and Mission*,
p. 147; see further the whole chapter on 'Liturgical Revision', pp. 142–55).

[3] 'Should we sing in the congregation, while in our daily lives we hardly
ever and hardly anywhere do that any longer en masse?' (Hoekendijk, *op.
cit.*, p. 76).

to be what it was in the beginning. It can create a kind of bridge between the local culture and Christian worship whose structure is foreign to that culture, but it can never remove the basic difference. Hence what was at first an adaptation to local culture becomes something simply borrowed. The same could be said about local dances.

To attempt to adapt Christian worship to a local culture by borrowing elements from it can lead to an *impasse*. Christian worship in its very essence is *profane*. It does not recognize the holiness of places, objects or rites. The 'holy' communion is so ordinary a meal that Paul had to remind the Corinthians that it is a commemoration of the death of the Lord until he comes (I Cor. 11.26). Later Christian worship was sacralized and so came to resemble other forms of worship. It has needed the Reformation of the sixteenth century and the lay movement of the last decades to set it free from its sacral overtones.

If we take notice of this, then we should attempt to promote cultural adaptation by borrowing elements from those traditions that have become profane and common and not from those that remain clearly sacralized. The early Christians did not take Jewish synagogues or Graeco-Roman temples as models for their churches; instead they adopted the basilica which was used as a law court or as a market or for meetings of various kinds. If we followed their example, we should build churches today like similar public buildings, we should use popular music and we should proceed in this way with regard to all the aspects of Christian worship and proclamation. In this way the risk of conservatism would be avoided,[1] because those cultural traditions that are common and profane adapt themselves much more quickly to change than do sacred traditions.

An important feature in public worship is the final blessing. Basically this is a form of dismissal or sending. It is addressed to Christians assembled together at the very moment when they are about to disperse and regain their places in the world where they have to render their daily acts of witness. This dismissal is

[1] See above, p. 14.

then a weekly dedication. The blessing of missionaries, according to the practice of certain missionary societies, is also connected with this final dismissal. While most of those present return to their normal place of work, the missionaries will have to cross cultural, linguistic and racial frontiers and will have to witness in new and often difficult circumstances. The Church calls down upon them a special blessing from God for the new work ahead of them and symbolizes it by the laying-on of hands.[1]

Worship gathers the Church together, the Church which has as its mission a dynamic presence in the world in the service of others. The order of its services should therefore reflect this dynamism, just as its readiness to exist for others should enable the worshippers to be aware of themselves as a separate body according to the will of God and both the sign and instrument of his coming Kingdom.[2]

(b) Word and Service

If the essential form of the Church's witness in the world is *presence*, in the sense defined above, we still have to consider the *modes* of this presence. The bible reminds us that the witness which God expects from his children in the world consists of both words and actions. These two modes of witness are so complementary that it would be wrong to give either a priority or to separate them from one another. Words and actions, proclamation and service, are like the two halves of an ellipse; they form a single whole. Sometimes the ellipse is termed 'word', but we have to acknowledge that word includes actions, as in the Prologue of St John: 'The Word became flesh and dwelt among us ... we have beheld his glory' (1.14). In the bible, the word is extraordinarily active. It creates, it establishes relations, it

[1] 'Receive now in the sight of this congregation (and of the representatives of the churches and parishes to which you belong) the encouragement and promise of the divine blessing which you need for the work to which you have pledged yourselves' (Basel Mission).

[2] *Cf.* 'Worship is not something that happens between the church and God, but between the world and God, the church being no more than an instrument. The church worships, in Christ, on behalf of the world, and indeed as the world (pro-existence, firstfruits, etc.).' *Planning for Mission*, p. 187.

provides nourishment, because it is life. But the ellipse can be termed 'service' (*diakonia*).[1] It is Paul especially who uses this term; for him everything, even preaching, is service. He has not always been followed in this; indeed since the Reformation 'ministry' (*diakonia*) is almost always understood to refer to preaching. Luther gave preaching an absolute priority.[2] Paul is not afraid to use the same word (*diakonia*) for the collection on behalf of the Jerusalem Church (II Cor. 8.4; 9.1, 12) and in Acts 6 it refers to the 'service of tables' and preaching, and this shows the close relationship there is between these two forms of witness. The first missionaries, who went out with the sole intention of preaching the Gospel, soon found that proclamation is a ministry (*diakonia*) which involves both word and action. As a consequence of this realization, the new communities underwent a harmonious and relatively complete development so that teaching, care and professional formation were naturally part of the preaching of the Gospel. But what intuition and practical work unite is often divided by theology; hence ministries, other than those of preaching and evangelism, have come to be regarded as auxiliaries. This false theology of

[1] *Cf.* Hoekendijk's definition of *diakonia*: 'When in the New Testament the total work of the offices is summed up as *diakonia*, it is simply impossible that the function of a president or speaker was meant thereby. The word points more in the direction of the work a waiter does, rendering service in an inconspicuous way' (*op. cit.*, p. 100). To Hoekendijk this service is 'useful – not per se necessary'. The offices are relativized as a matter of principle, yet they are given to the Church as 'the extra that God cannot help but give over and above that which is necessary. Perhaps we get closest to it when we accept *the offices* as a *gracious surplus*' (*ibid.*, p. 101). Later he says: 'If we would think that we can easily do without this extra assistance, we overestimate ourselves and fail to appreciate God's liberality, according to which he wants to care for his people "more than abundantly" and therefore has intended them to receive a gracious surplus' (*ibid.*, p. 102).

[2] Luther was not consistent in his translation. Acts 6.1: *Versorgung* = providing for. Acts 11.29; 12.25: *Gabe* = help or relief. Acts 21.19; Rom. 15.31; I Cor. 16.15; Heb. 1.14; Rev. 2.19: *Dienst* = ministry. II Cor. 8.4; 9.1, 12: *Liebeswerk* = work of charity. II Cor. 11.8: *dienen* = to minister to. Luther uses *Amt*, meaning ministry, 17 times and *Versorgung*, *Gabe* and *Liebeswerk* 13 times. His bias appears in II Cor. 5.18 which he translates 'the ministry that *preaches* reconciliation' whereas the Greek text simply says 'the ministry of reconciliation'.

ministries has had serious consequences for traditional missionary work and for the diaconal work of the Church.

Primary and Auxiliary Ministries

'Auxiliary ministry' can mean two quite different things. On the one hand, an auxiliary ministry can be regarded as a useful but inessential support for a primary ministry; in which case the efficacy of an auxiliary ministry will be judged, not by its own proper criteria, but by the extent to which it contributes or fails to contribute to the expansion of the Church. Since this type of ministry is usually costly, it is often threatened with suppression; it then defends itself by attempting to prove that it is necessary by presenting statistics and arguing that many baptisms derive from it. This kind of argument was very widespread in Africa, especially in relation to Christian schools, so that they have come to be regarded as one of the most effective instruments for the expansion of the Church. It is therefore not surprising that competition between different Churches has been most evident in the realm of education.

On the other hand, an auxiliary ministry has been understood as one that is useful for the general development of the community or of a people, for whom the Church accepts responsibility until such time as the state can take it over. The consequence is that this form of ministry is then regarded in a rather detached way and every opportunity is taken to hand it over to the state in order to be set free for 'more essential' tasks. This is in general the attitude of missions in Asia, and especially in India, to schools. At the beginning of this century the argument in their defence was advanced that they had a permeating influence, but this lost its validity when it was realized that unquestioned influence did not prepare the pupils to receive the message of the Gospel but speeded up their secularization.[1]

Interested and Disinterested Service

With good reason the tendency to consider so-called auxiliary ministries (schools, hospitals) as means for the expansion of the

[1] On the problem of schools in India see J. Rossel, 'Wissen und Gewissheit' in *Wir lieben Indien*, Bad Salzuflen 1963.

Church has been condemned, and at the same time it has been pointed out that they are to be judged essentially in the light of their immediate aims (health and education). In this way they have been separated from evangelism and given their own particular status. This tendency has made much progress over the past twenty years and has given rise to the creation of independent service organizations (Cimade, EPER, Dienst in Uebersee, Church World Service, etc.); they are devoted to what is called disinterested service, as distinct from that of missions, which is said to be interested. The result of all this is an unfortunate confusion which needs to be resolved by the leaders of these organizations and of missions.

We must emphasize once more that to regard these service ministries as useful instruments for the expansion of the Church is to endorse a false theology.[1] Nevertheless, with some exceptions, most missionaries have regarded the service rendered by schools and hospitals as 'disinterested', in the sense that they did not concern themselves with whether or not they contributed to the expansion of the Church. The love that they announced in their proclamation compelled them to interfere in secular affairs.[2] Theological justification, as is normal, followed on this interference.

We must also acknowledge that the radical separation between mission and service also derives from a false theology. Actions are opposed to words, 'disinterested' service to the 'interested' mission, to such an extent that social action has replaced evangelism, and service for its simple humanitarian value is said to be the modern form of the Church's mission.

[1] 'It is important to stress that this suffering service, this *diakonia*, is not an instrument of mission. All kinds of service, such as medical work, are embodiments of the Gospel; they are signs not means. It is not through these acts of service that God establishes his Kingdom; rather these acts of service are witnesses to its present reality' (Davies, *Worship and Mission*, p. 34). This is an interesting distinction that needs further study. Are signs of God's action not also instruments of his action?

[2] 'Necessity alone will lead a missionary to interfere in secular affairs' – these words, uttered at a missionary conference in New York in 1900, are quoted by N. Goodall, *Christian Missions and Social Ferment*, p. 13. See the whole of his chapter entitled 'Interfering in the Secular', pp. 13–36.

Since there is much misunderstanding about what is 'interested' and what is 'disinterested', we must examine these two terms carefully. We have seen that Christ is not disinterested. If he gives his life to the world, this is not for nothing; it is in order that the world may have life; it is for its salvation, for its reconciliation with its Creator, for its share in the covenant which is offered to it. The Christian similarly is not disinterested. His act of witness, by word and deed, has a definite goal. This is what is meant by the tiny word 'for' in *The Church for Others*.[1] To be for others does not just mean to be with others. Identification with one's neighbour only has meaning if it goes beyond the condition of the neighbour and leads him towards the goal which has prompted the identification. This goal is to enable the neighbour to share in the righteousness of the Kingdom of God; it is to seek with him and for him how and where God gives him this righteousness now. To be for others is to be with them in order to integrate them into the Kingdom which is coming; it is to seek with them how and where this Kingdom is incarnating itself today, how and where God is at work today 'reconciling the world to himself'. It is to discern and identify with them and for them the present signs of his Kingdom and of his righteousness. In other words, when we say 'for others', we do not understand solely doing something for them in the social or political sphere, but also communicating to them the faith which actuates us. If we do not behave in this way, we are guilty of a grave omission. It is as if we gave them bread to support them in life without speaking about life; as if we gave them a medicine without explaining its effects; as if we were bringing them into a forward march without indicating the reason for it or its goal. It is a serious omission, even a cruel one, because in this way we lead others to believe that the moon is made of green cheese, to regard penultimate things as the ultimate. To serve without explaining the meaning of our service is as serious as preaching the Gospel without fulfilling the service it proclaims.

[1] This is the title of the North American and West European Working Groups' Report on the 'Missionary Structure of the Congregation' (Geneva 1966).

If we should communicate to our neighbour the faith which directs the service we render him, we should also rejoice when this faith is accepted and shared by him and we should receive him with joy into the community of believers.

It is wrong to exert pressure upon anyone. Nor can we deny that pressure has indeed been exerted, but we should not generalize. The most faithful missionaries have been those who have respected the liberty of others, for it is this liberty that constitutes the basis of the covenant which God offers to men. It would, however, be wrong to give up witnessing to our faith by performing acts of service because we fear there may be a misunderstanding. Misunderstanding is always possible; it is the task of preaching to remove it.

The Motives of Witness

The history of missions shows that there are two motives above all others which have been employed to justify mission: the saving of souls and the planting of Churches.[1] We would be wrong to reject these motives, whose fault is simply that they are not complete.[2] They have been detached from the context of the

---

[1] See M. Linz, *Anwalt der Welt*, Stuttgart-Berlin 1964.

[2] To J. G. Davies these motives are not only defective but wrong, because they revolve around the Church conceived as the centre of mission (*Worship and Mission*, p. 49). Davies' criticism of defective concepts of mission (*ibid.*, pp. 35–69 and *Dialogue with the World*, pp. 40–57) is valid inasmuch as it is addressed to a Church that has totally discarded the New Testament concept of Church. In such a perspective Church extension makes no sense. But according to the New Testament concept of the Church (and I believe that our present Churches, in spite of their deviations, still do witness to this concept) it is meaningful. The Church is the growing company of those who have become partakers of Christ and as such do 'participate in his mission to the world' (*cf.* the section on the meaning of baptism in *Worship and Mission*, pp. 72–92). Davies agrees with van den Heuvel that 'the Church which preaches the Lordship of Christ and invites people to join him and them in Christ's own mission to the world cannot dominate or force people into belief. To do so would deny the heart of the Gospel which says that man encounters the living God and is challenged by him to decide whether to accept or reject this involvement in mission' (*Dialogue*, p. 48). Mission is ultimately God's call in Christ to participate in his new society. Since this new society is within the present one, there must be an inevitable clash between systems of ideas and values. This clash is resented by the

Gospel and consequently the distinctive character of the biblical message has been lost. To restrict salvation to souls is to forget that not only the soul but also the body is heir to the promise of resurrection (I Cor. 15), and that man is not just an individual but also a social being, so that the salvation to which he is called includes his social relationships.[1]

To restrict mission to the planting of Churches where none as yet exist is to forget that besides the gathering of those who have accepted the Gospel for edification and thanksgiving, the Church is on the march towards the Kingdom that is to come and must show this by its visible participation in the forward march of all mankind. The reality towards which we are going and which is proclaimed by the entire bible and for which Christ gave his life is more than the saving of souls, more than the gathering together of souls that have been saved, it is a Kingdom which stretches out to the totality of creation. This is why Jesus taught his disciples to pray: 'Thy Kingdom come'.

If we take account of all this, we may direct our attention to a sentence of Paul's which defines the motives of his missionary action: 'Him we proclaim, warning every man and teaching every man in wisdom, that we may present every man mature in Christ' (Col. 1.28). At a time when we are too ready to mouth generalizations – the mission of the Church, witness, presence in the world – it is necessary to remind ourselves that according to Paul the concrete task of Christians is to present mature in Christ all those on whose behalf he is present in the world. This

---

newly emerging African and Asian nations and is too often dismissed with a sweeping reference to proselytism. Though it is true that the herald 'makes known what has happened', it does not seem to me possible to renounce urging, exhorting and persuading (*cf. Worship and Mission*, p. 57), because, as Davies writes elsewhere: 'if the goal of mission is to enable men to be fully human, then we must be liberating agents, contagiously human, setting men free from servitude to false powers and false idols' (*Dialogue*, p. 15). I maintain therefore that the motives of winning souls for the Lamb or Church extension are not altogether wrong but defective, because they do justice only to parts of the biblical record but not to its fundamental emphasis upon the Kingdom and its righteousness.

[1] Paul shows this in I Cor. 7.14; John and James refer to it continually in their epistles; Jesus pronounces the beatitudes in the plural: 'Blessed are those . . .'.

maturity is not a moral maturity, as with the Stoics, nor a spiritual one, as with the Hindus. It is the maturity which is the consequence of being integrated into the great movement of the love of God towards all men and its goal is the communion of all, with one another and with God. It is therefore a maturity which concerns the relations of men with their Creator as well as their social relations: 'You shall love the Lord your God with all your heart, and with all your soul, and with all your mind. . . . You shall love your neighbour as yourself' (Matt. 22.37ff.). 'To be at the service of man, whoever he may be, is always in fact to open for him the doors of a fellowship where he will find a place.'[1] The goal of our action ought to be this: to allow others 'to find a place' in the great fellowship of God.

(c)   *The Organs of Execution*

Since the union of the International Missionary Council and the World Council of Churches in 1961, considerable efforts have been made to integrate Church and Mission at the regional and local level. Where a Church occupies the same geographical region as the headquarters of a missionary society, this integration is relatively simple. This is so with regard to the Dutch Churches and their missions. The integration of missionary societies attached to particular denominations is also easy, such as the missionary societies of the Presbyterian and Congregational Churches in the United States. In other countries, especially in Europe, the situation is much more complex. Certain large missionary societies, such as those of Paris and Basel, have a very wide basis and act in collaboration with a large number of Churches which are territorially distinct or have doctrinal differences. The Basel Mission is related to twenty-seven Churches made up of four nationalities, without counting the Churches with which it collaborates in Asia and Africa.[2] Integration is not possible in these circumstances unless both Churches and Missions are regrouped. This regrouping has taken place in Switzerland between the Moravian Mission,

[1] J. Beaumont in *Vers une église pour les autres*, p. 161.
[2] Nineteen Swiss Churches, five German, two French and one Austrian.

the Basel Mission, the Paris Mission, the Swiss Mission in South Africa, the Mission in Eastern Asia, the Gospel Mission on the Nile, the Protestant Mission of Belgium and Christian Action in the East.[1] The collaboration between these societies has been carried to great lengths. They have a common budget, while at the same time allowing their contributors to give either for a designated purpose or to the general account. In French-speaking Switzerland they have carried the integration further in that seven Churches support a Missionary Department to which they have delegated the exercise of their apostolic function.[2] The success of this new structure will depend upon the way in which this delegation works in practice. Here we encounter the major problem in the structures of modern society, in which *delegation* has an important part to play. Delegation is an art which we have still to learn how to put

[1] See E. Blum, *Die Mission der reformierten Schweiz*, Basel 1965.

[2] The Churches concerned are the National Protestant Church of Geneva, the Evangelical Free Church of Geneva, the Evangelical Reformed Church of the Canton of Vaud, the Evangelical Reformed Church of the Canton of Neuchâtel, the Evangelical Reformed Church of the Canton of Berne, the Reformed Church of the Canton of Fribourg (French-language parishes) and the Evangelical Reformed Church of Valais.

The preamble to the act constituting the Missionary Department affirms: 'The Protestant Churches of French-speaking Switzerland, recognizing that the missionary societies have aroused and sustained within their parishes the wish to participate in the evangelization of the world and believing, with those Churches that are attached to the World Council, that since they are the objects of the divine grace in Jesus Christ they are also witnesses among the nations and must themselves assume this missionary function in countries beyond the sea, convinced that the present situation in the world demands from them an increased obedience and a greater unity of action, have decided to establish a Missionary Department whose goal is to support the proclamation of the Gospel of Jesus Christ throughout the whole world "in order that all men may believe in him and be saved"' (the Constitution of the Commission of Mission and Evangelism of the WCC. The Missionary Department, which was created in 1963, has accepted responsibility for Transvaal and Mozambique and has become the instrument of liaison between the Churches listed above and the missionary societies which do not have headquarters in French-speaking Switzerland, i.e. all the missions referred to except the Swiss Mission in South Africa who has given up its separate existence. The Missionary Department is directed by a missionary synod composed of members nominated by the Churches.

into practice. To delegate is to pass on responsibilities without abandoning them.

At the request of the Basel Mission, the German Churches of the South-west[1] have undertaken missionary work in common. The German branch of the Basel Mission, which has its headquarters at Stuttgart, is in direct contact with this, but since the lines of communication with the Churches of Africa and Asia pass through Basel, the Churches of the South-west are also involved in Basel itself.

At the present time the integration of Mission and Church in South-west Europe takes the form of a number of jigsaw pieces, several of which fit easily together while others have little correspondence. The integration of Mission and Church demands regroupings and new concentrations of effort which will quickly move outside the area where they have come into being.

It is, however, the will to integrate that is more important than structures; but this will is not always well directed.

The 'integrists', for example, base their understanding upon inadequate structures and forget that we no longer live in the epoch of *cujus regio, ejus religio*; we are in fact in the midst of pluralism. Churches and missions have to re-examine their structures in terms of today and not of the past. The regional and centralizing ideas of the integrists have to be left behind. Our pluralist society with its plural values has many centres and its structures have to correspond. This means that these structures must be opened up, for we should not be afraid of several nuclei in our churchly and missionary structures, although we should be careful not to produce too many and therefore should direct our attention in the first instance to the task of regrouping Churches and missionary societies. The regrouping of the Churches in French-speaking Switzerland is a first step forward; it shows the way, but it is still far from the goal to be achieved in Switzerland as a whole, as well as in France, Belgium, Austria and South-west Germany. We must also co-ordinate these

[1] Württemberg, Baden, the Palatinate, Hesse, Nassau and Kurhessen-Waldeck.

various centres. This is not simply a technical question; it is above all a matter of individuals. Neither the copying of letters nor the spreading of information will be sufficient; there must be person to person contact to provide the necessary lubrication for the complicated wheels of modern administrative machinery. Above all we must take into account the fact that the Church is the living organism of the living God; it has always been very diverse and it has never been possible to enclose it within a single system. It is watched over by the Spirit who apportions his *charismata* as he wills. We should, however, pay serious attention to these gifts; to be endowed with a particular gift is to be invested with a clearly defined responsibility within a fixed area. Since mission close at hand is just as important as mission far away, there is no need for a single organism to carry out the two. The setting up of a single structure in one place may be right in certain circumstances but wrong in others. The rule to be followed is *multum, non multa*. We need to have organisms that concentrate upon certain special questions, while still remaining in contact with all other forms of structure. From this point of view, the directive function of the Church is to be seen less and less as that of preparing measures, reaching decisions about them and putting them into effect, and more and more inspiring and co-ordinating the specialist organisms. Amongst these are of course the missionary societies, whose task is not to embody the total mission of the Church – they would be insufficient for this – but to fulfil a precise task across the geographical, cultural and racial frontiers of the Churches which provide their point of departure. This special apostolic function is only a small part of the apostolic function of the Church as a whole; it is moreover a difficult function to perform because it is less obvious than many others and because it requires a very high degree of specialization.

Missionary Involvement

THE MISSION of the Church in and for the world is accomplished through service (*diakonia*, ministry), and this service is both proclamation and action. All the members of the Church are 'agents' of this service in different ways; they are therefore all missionaries. The false division between clergy and laity, which was abolished in principle by the Reformation, is now being replaced by a valid distinction between those members that are entrusted with the *general mission* of the Church and those that have *special missions*: deacons, deaconesses, social workers, administrators, catechists, pastors, missionaries (in the traditional sense of the term), who carry out different tasks outside their cultural *milieu*.

Ordinary and Extraordinary Ministries

Although we now acknowledge, more than ever before, the general mission of the Church with which all members are entrusted, many still see their role as essentially passive and regard specialists as those primarily called upon to execute mission. At the opposite extreme, there are those who seek the disappearance of specialists and specialized institutions in order to force all the members of the Church to recognize their responsibilities.[1] Those who support this drastic remedy have a somewhat questionable understanding of the Church. They tend

[1] 'Special groups are faced with a twofold danger. Because of their very existence and of the work they undertake, the Church tends to find excuses for evading its proper responsibilities and so neglects its unchanging task and uses these groups as substitutes for what it ought to be doing but is not doing. On the other hand, these groups are in danger of regarding themselves as alone constituting the true Church' (*L'Eglise dans son rôle diaconal au sein de la société contemporaine*, COE. Geneva 1966, p. 61).

to identify the Church with the organized institution and they consider that everything that is not under the control of its regional organs is not really of the Church. This 'diocesan' idea, inherited from Constantinian times, fails to take account of the dynamism of contemporary society and it appears to forget that the Spirit blows wherever he wills. We must recognize that members of the Church have a right to join together to perform those particular tasks which their faith and love dictate to them; we ought even to encourage them so that a rapid and effective response can be made to the changing conditions of our social life; the task of regional organizations would then be to coordinate these separate and special activities in the best way possible and in the general interests of the Church as a whole.

This is not only true of institutions that come into being through Christians joining together, but it is also applicable to specialized ministries. The Church of the New Testament is aware of special ministries over and above the general ministry; both are necessary to ensure the life of the Church as a corporate whole. When Paul and Barnabas are sent on a mission by the Church at Antioch, they are separated for a special task which cannot be undertaken by all the members of that Church. The members of the Church, who are charged with its general mission, must always delegate certain tasks to specialists or to specialized organizations. The important thing is to preserve a close contact, as at Antioch, between the 'ordinary' members and the 'extraordinary' ones.

If specialization is a necessity in the present age, it is also demanded by the Spirit, who has always been the author of special vocations, even though the Church has been tempted to impede them. This is why so many special vocations have had to be carried out outside the official framework of the Church. We must therefore take care that, in attributing importance to the general ministry of the Church, those extraordinary ministries that it needs are not neglected.

Direct and Indirect Compassion

What is the meaning for the Christian of the obligation to witness where he lives and works? Is the general ministry of the Christian limited to his personal relations within his work or should it include certain aspects of that work? The divine compassion, of which we are the object, draws us out of ourselves towards our neighbour, in such a way that in taking our place by his side and in identifying ourselves with his situation we become *his* neighbour. The impulse of love or compassion which we bear to another enables *my* neighbour to find *his* neighbour in me. It is to this reversal of the situation that Jesus refers at the end of the parable of the Good Samaritan: 'Which of these three, do you think, proved neighbour to the man who fell among robbers?' (Luke 10.36).

In order to be a neighbour charged with a mission, it is not enough to identify oneself with the situation of the person or persons towards whom we are borne by love; it is also necessary 'to save' them; we have to transfer them from their situation into another better one. It would have been very touching and quite useless for the Good Samaritan to have sat himself down beside the man who had fallen among robbers and to have been satisfied with merely bringing him 'a presence', even if such an action involved the possibility that he would be stripped in his turn. Yet this is apparently what some people mean when they talk about identification. But identification and presence are not ends in themselves; they are the instruments of a transformation, of a change, of salvation. The Good Samaritan becomes the neighbour of him who fell among robbers not just because he stopped by his side but because he bound up his wounds, set him on his own beast and provided him with food and shelter at an inn. To be a constructive neighbour, our love must be according to the image of the love of God. This is embodied in the covenant which is the offering of perfect communion.[1] Our action must then be an introduction to that communion, which becomes immediately possible through the obedience of faith

[1] See above, pp. 83ff.

and will one day be evident to the eyes of everyone. This communion – and nothing else – is the true salvation; it is the admitted or unacknowledged goal of all Christian service. When we become a neighbour to someone else and we identify ourselves with his situation and take steps to help him to go beyond it, then the measures we adopt to achieve this are stages towards a definite goal. They are stages which show that in its intention the creation is good and that despite its shortcomings it has before it a fulfilment which has already begun.

When he tries to be a constructive neighbour, the Christian is faced with three problems. The first concerns motives. From the moment that we regard Christian action in the service of one's neighbour (health, education, professional training) as a stage on the way to the perfect communion of men with God and of men with one another, we are in conflict with those who charge us with a failure to be disinterested. A statement which has been recently issued by an African state has emphasized that 'the medical work of Christian organizations is not an instrument of evangelism. It is the expression of the Christian ideal of brotherly love towards all God's creatures.' This love, it must be stated, surpasses the strictly physical needs of those that are sick; beyond their health, it is aimed towards their salvation.[1] Their regaining of health is only a stage on the way which *can* lead those that are ill to be integrated by faith into that perfect communion which is offered by Jesus Christ to all men; the Church is the sign of this communion. It is of course clear that no material or moral pressure should be used to attain this end. But are Christians really required to look after the sick without showing them where they may find perfect health or without declaring to them the good news of complete health in a restored communion or without opening to them the doors of a brotherhood in which they will find a place?[2] The Hindu Minister of Planning in the Indian Republic, in an address to Christians of all confessions who had come together to co-ordinate their part in the struggle against hunger, has insisted

[1] *Eglise et guérison*, WCC, Geneva 1965.
[2] See above, p. 83.

that in addition to being experts they must also be the sowers of hope.[1] How can this be done, if Christians do not declare the reasons for their hope?

We have seen above[2] that we are faced with a serious confusion between evangelism and proselytism. Evangelism is an act of proclamation and a summons combined with an invitation. Proselytism seeks to force a decision by any means whatsoever; it is interested in numbers, whereas evangelism leaves the increase of the Church to the action of the Holy Spirit.

By the side of this old problem we must set another which is the result of the revolutionary development of our society; this is the problem of the *dimensions* of Christian action. Until now this action has been limited to works of charity – as regards health, this has meant the care of the sick, and the aged and infirm; as regards society, it has meant first-aid, looking after orphans, supporting rehabilitation centres. There have, however, been two noticeable exceptions to this limitation, viz. commercial and industrial undertakings fostered by certain missions and then handed over to private societies, and also schools.[3] These

[1] AIKYIA, July 1966. A monthly magazine for students published in India by the Student Christian Movement.

[2] See p. 95.

[3] Norman Goodall, *Christian Missions and Social Ferment*, 1964, pp. 13–20. 'The picture here is one of more than hunger and its appeasement. Behind the hunger, in this instance, was the caste system of India. The empty stomachs were those of outcaste converts. By their acceptance of Christianity they had cut themselves off even from the meagre subsistence which had been theirs as the lowest of the low in the many strata of a complex social structure. What was to be done about it? Clearly the 'poor-house', even under Christian auspices, could not – in the opinion of the missionary – go deep enough. "This would be neither business-like nor just and, furthermore, it would be demoralizing", said a speaker at the same conference in 1900. The remedy was employment and a fair wage, and it was this that the missionary societies had sought to provide.

'The story had begun nearly half a century earlier. Its setting was South London and the society was the Basel Mission whose headquarters are in Switzerland. While mainly supported by the Swiss Churches, the Society has always drawn support and recruited its missionaries from other European countries besides Switzerland, and especially from Germany. In two of its great fields of service – West Africa and India – it pioneered in what became known as "industrial missions", the most successful enterprises being those in Mangarlore, South India' (*op. cit.*, pp. 13f.).

industrial plants and these schools both show that Christian action is not limited to after-care. Nevertheless even in these undertakings Christian action is essentially a personal expression of love.[1] It is above all in person to person contact that Christians believe they must witness, but these relations, however important they may be, are not complete in themselves. We shall appreciate this more readily if we return to the problem presented to us by the forward march of the young folk of Bali.[2] Education takes place within personal relations; for the master to teach he must be in contact with his students; it is this human contact that is the principal attraction of being an educator. But when the educator has to concern himself with his students' future, it is no longer sufficient; to unite school and life there has to be a different relation which certain theologians have termed an indirect relation.[3] This relation replaces person to person contact by organization. The students have to be directed towards certain professions and hence training centres for these have to be set up. Christians cannot do this on their own, but only as members of a society to which they belong and in which they work.[4]

[1] 'Even when the rhetoric has passed, the tale continues to read impressively. It is one of brave endeavour and ingenuity; elation with success was always quickly tempered by failure. There were embarrassments and misunderstandings in plenty and many goodwill ships foundered. But countless individuals were helped to a more tolerable way of life, with some easing of the struggle for existence and some mitigation of the penalties exacted by ancient social orders from those who broke out of the pattern by their conversion to Christianity. More and more, however, Christian missions were, along this road, interfering in the secular. Tiny as the inroads upon the established order might be, they were being made and their effect was cumulative. Not the least of the by-products of all this were the quickening of aspiration and the implied, if not direct, criticism of the prevailing patterns of society. The primary object of all this missionary experimentation was the individual, not the social order. The most persistent motive was concern for the person. But the necessity which compelled the "interference" was itself part of an inescapable involvement in society' (Norman Goodall, *op. cit.*, pp. 19f.).

[2] See above, pp. 1–4.

[3] See above, pp. 23f., for a preliminary discussion of this problem.

[4] This does not mean that within the fellowship of the Church personal relations should not always have pre-eminence over indirect relations. For

Social aid is not only concerned with bringing direct help to the most people, it is also concerned to attack evil at its roots in a more effective manner than does personal assistance. Hence Christian action extends beyond the confines of person to person relations in order to be open to social relations. The Christian has to act on two levels at once, on the level of love 'which knows no mediation'[1] and on the level of indirect relations, i.e. on the level of social structures.[2]

The ordinary member of the Church who is invited to enter into Christian involvement in widely differing spheres is exceedingly ill-prepared for this task, and so it is not surprising if his involvement is more verbal than specific. It is in connexion with this that the existing service institutions (groups of deacons and deaconesses, missionary societies and inter-aid organizations) may be of assistance to the Church because of their mediating position between Christian personal action (casework) and Christian social action (community development)

'the law of Christ is love, and love in its fullness and truth always shows itself in a personal encounter, within a personal relationship. Love knows no mediation.' Nevertheless, 'modern society itself could not be satisfied with a purely personal expression of love and mutual help'. It must organize mutual help, social security and social services in such a way that help is provided for those in need. In our anonymous systems 'technique wins over the personal act of sympathy and love. This is the price of efficiency. And yet the direct and the indirect relationships are not entirely heterogeneous' (R. Mehl in *Christian Social Ethics in a Changing World*, 1966, pp. 54f.).

[1] *ibid., loc. cit.*

[2] The report on the ministerial role of the Church in contemporary society uses the term *diakonia* or ministry in a very wide sense to include 'the active plan of God to help those who suffer and to meet the needs of individuals by establishing a life of justice and dignity for all his creatures' (*L'Eglise dans son rôle diaconal au sein de la société contemporaine*, p. 12). This very full definition is in agreement with the concerns of the Conference on 'Church and Society'. At the end of a very detailed study of governmental social services, the report on the ministerial role of the Church concludes: 'The Churches will seek to collaborate in order to establish the best possible kind of society, in which everyone will have the opportunity to develop to the maximum according to the gifts which God accords him and to bring to the whole of society his greatest contribution. This means that the Churches should be in touch with every aspect of social life and of social justice in such a way that they can take an active part in the improvement of society' (*op. cit.*, p. 54).

and their need to recruit and train the necessary personnel.[1] The Rev. L. Cooke appreciates very clearly the dilemma in which many Christians find themselves at present: 'If on the one hand Christians are convinced of the duty that the Gospel lays upon them to help and to heal those in need, it is also true on the other hand that they are not clear about their role in modern states and the need to work for the good of all on different political and social bases.'[2]

The obligation to extend Christian action into the social sphere presents the Christian with a third problem, i.e. that of co-operating in the political and social fields with men who profess a different faith or none at all. The Church and Society Conference saw this very clearly.[3]

Christians must adopt a positive attitude towards those who are working for the general welfare. 'We honour all those, whether Christian or not, who are working actively to redeem their societies.' Nevertheless, the particular function of the Christian within social development is just as evident: 'In every circumstance, the Christian is called actively to seek reconciliation where there is tension, justice where there is injustice, freedom where there is bondage, and opportunity where this is denied.'[4]

It was not to be expected that a Conference, such as the one on Church and Society, could have considered in great detail the complex problem of the co-operation of people of different religions, but there is a useful hint in a section devoted to the

[1] 'The primary agents of the dialogue must be the lay members of the Church in their diverse social roles and functions, with the ordained minister performing the part of an "enabler", assisting the laity in what is essentially *their* dialogue. The focus of this dialogue is the bearing of the Gospel on the world, i.e. the attempt to discover the reality of the justifying and reconciling action of God in Christ in the context of particular situations which are shared alike by Christians and non-Christians' (J. G. Davies, *Dialogue with the World*, 1967, pp. 6of.). Davies adds an interesting example: 'A Christian in industry, for example, should regard it as his primary duty to attend the branch meetings of his trade union rather than some Church organization.'

[2] *L'Eglise dans son rôle diaconal*, p. 3.

[3] *World Conference on Church and Society*, Geneva 1967, pp. 52–5.

[4] *ibid.*, p. 135.

development of the missionary structures of the Church: 'Such structures should be capable of including and relating to those who are unable to make credal affirmations, but who can see the secular significance of what are in fact theological truths.'[1] We have suggested above that the co-operation of Christians with people of other faiths is possible in so far as their different faith is parallel to the Christian faith. In such circumstances Christians and non-Christians find themselves more or less on the same ground because they share similar general views about man and social development. This parallelism provides great opportunities for the Christian but can also lead him to turn away from his biblical faith towards a more secular faith, and this in its turn could result ultimately in a complete indifference and even in nihilism. In this situation the Christian should remind himself constantly of the warning of Christ: 'if salt has lost its taste, how shall its saltness be restored? It is no longer good for anything except to be thrown out and trodden under foot by men' (Matt. 5.13).

Involvement beyond Geographical and Cultural Frontiers

We have devoted the major part of this study to the mission of the Church and to the general missionary involvement of its members because this is necessary; we cannot consider specific and limited action until we have a view of the whole. The missionary pioneers of the last century neglected this too much. Each one, moved by the Spirit, set out without concerning himself overmuch with either what others had already accomplished or with the relationship of his activity to the Church's mission in general. Yet the second half of the twentieth century may well turn out to be a period of great syntheses and of co-ordination pushed so far that it absorbs the greater part of the forces necessary for action. Our generation is so fascinated by a vision of the whole that it is sometimes afraid to engage in the specific and the limited.

[1] *ibid.*, p. 181.

While it is, of course, necessary to relate everything to the whole, it is equally important to move from the general to the particular. The Church does not execute its mission in a void; it is always encountering men who belong to a particular race or culture, men who live within fixed geographical and political frontiers and who have reached a certain stage of development and are grappling with specific problems.

We must now turn to the question of the mission in which we of the West are still required to engage today in Africa, Asia and Latin America. We should also have in mind the mission which Christians in Africa, Asia and Latin America are called to fulfil in the West. If we do not examine this latter mission, that is because it is a task beyond our competence, so we shall confine ourselves to the mission of Western Christians outside their own frontiers.

The Handicaps of the Western Missionaries

Today the Western Christian who thinks about the subject and is aware of his responsibilities has replaced his former superiority complex by a loss of confidence in himself. He bears the burden of the shortcomings of his ancestors: colonialism, exploitation, racialism, aggressiveness, desire for gain, religious arrogance, intellectual self-sufficiency and cultural imperialism. He tries to overcome this inheritance by embracing humility and by identifying himself with the victims of his predatory forerunners. This identification is something far more than simply a verbal one; it is often so complete as to paralyse the Western Christian both in action and proclamation. He then undergoes a crisis of disillusionment. Despite all the limitations he imposes upon himself and the humiliations he is ready to accept, he is still regarded by many non-Whites as a 'terrible colonialist' or a 'terrible imperialist'. This disillusionment which is experienced by all young Westerners going to Africa, Asia or South America with the intention of giving themselves whole-heartedly to service is for some a salutary crisis from which they emerge stronger, but for others, unfortunately, it leads to cynicism. But these cynics cut themselves off from the community that is devoted to compassion and is motivated by it; they cut themselves off from the Church of Christ and help to increase the obstacles to a drawing together of peoples and races.

The Colonial Past

The Western missionary easily thinks that his Christian understanding of service will enable him to overcome his racial handicap, but this is a mistake that must be avoided. Although, thanks to God, service carried out in the obedience of faith always bears fruit anew, so that hatred, amongst other evils, is being overcome, we have not yet reached the day when we can say that it is no longer true that 'the fathers have eaten sour grapes, and the children's teeth are set on edge' (Jer. 31.29). There is a solidarity in history from which we cannot escape. The Western Christian, who engages in mission beyond his own frontiers, must therefore accept his solidarity with a colonial history for which he is not directly responsible and he must bear this, because only that which is borne can be finally purified and transformed. This is the meaning of the message of the cross and of Jesus' summons to his disciples to carry their cross.

Affluence

Identification has its limits. These limits do not necessarily depend upon our own choice nor upon the weakness of our bodies. If we so wish, we can adapt ourselves to the 'primitiveness' of the man of the Stone Age; we can put up with accommodation like his; we can dress alike and exist like him by cultivating millet, and we can appreciate his art. But all this would, in his eyes, be completely useless and he would soon tell us so, because the Gospel which we announce to him opens up new spiritual and material horizons towards which he wants us to lead him. We have to bear our wealth which is measured not simply by our personal possessions but by our belonging to that hemisphere which is itself rich in comparison with the rest of the world. It is by no means easy to be forgiven for being rich nor for having been rich, for wealth creates envy. When this is not so, we must recognize the grace of God and see this as an anticipation and sign of his coming Kingdom; this is a gift we have not deserved.[1]

Knowledge and Experience

The wounds inflicted by colonialism are disappearing day by day. Wealth is not always with us; we leave it in part behind us. But our knowledge and our experience are always there, as long as work lasts, even if we do not make them felt. In this knowledge and experience there is a superiority which is painful for others even when they themselves need them. This handicap is one of the most serious which Western missionaries have to face, but it can be reduced to the extent that Westerners are called not just to posts in which they are *still* indispensable but to service with Africans and Asiatics who have the same knowledge and who are sometimes more experienced than they. Although this occasionally happens in the realm of theology, it is very rare in teaching or technology. Moreover, immigration laws usually require from foreigners qualifications which are superior to the general level in the country and this too makes

[1] We should do well to heed the challenge of J. C. Hoekendijk: 'If we want to take our normal place in the world community, we shall have to carry through to its conclusion the disenchantment (*Entzauberung*) of Europe, the West, from myth to quite ordinary continent. This means also that we have to give up our privileged positions: our "domination" (in this respect much has already been done) and our "wealth" (in this respect I think we have still to begin). The world of tomorrow, seen as a whole, can only be a *poor* world. For the moment, one cannot yet reckon on "welfare for all". Assistance to countries of rapid social change can only very modestly aim at "raising the standard *toward* poverty"; it can only just help to pass the threshold of man-worthy (but still pauper) existence; at best, a minimum existence for all can be reached. Solidarity with this world, therefore, can be nothing else than solidarity in poverty. And the genuineness of our desire for this must be proved in the self-discipline that we dare to impose upon ourselves: our restriction of ourselves to a minimum and our readiness to share liberally with others all that is at our disposal. To my mind, this demands of the church that it empty itself to become the church-of-the-poor' (*The Church Inside Out*, 1966, pp. 179f.).

the problem no easier. Yet these highly qualified services are precisely the ones that are needed by the states in the Third World. The Western Christian may be helped to bear these handicaps through the existence of a Christian community which he is invited to join.[1]

Leaving One's Own Country

The missionary gives a particular value to his mission by the effort he makes, when going to a foreign country, to learn the language, the culture and, as far as possible, the ways of thinking of those amongst whom he has come to serve. This effort makes him a bridge between two cultures. The Christian in a foreign country has as his mission the unification of that which tends to break apart. He must remind men of their universal vocation in Christ; this is a most arduous task and it would be wrong to attempt to silence him. He who is the bridge between two races belongs entirely to neither one nor the other, because the effort to become familiar with a foreign language so as to declare the Gospel in it often results in a decreased study of one's own language. Moreover, despite all his efforts, he will speak the new language with some trace of an accent that will betray his origins. But the presence of 'bridge-members' between races is essential for the Church in order that it may declare and reveal its universality. It is essential for races, too, that these contacts should be enriched in order to save them from a sterile isolation. It is also necessary for the world as a whole so that it may become more united.

In order to lay the foundation of his people, God made Abraham a foreigner. His descendants were foreigners in Egypt and, after their deliverance, they lived among the Canaanites, once more as foreigners since they could neither share in their worship nor be assimilated to them. Today God still lays a specific mission upon his children who are foreigners twice over – foreigners because of their Christian vocation and

[1] See what has been said about Christian presence as a *visit* and about the tact with which Paul prepared for his visit to Rome (Rom. 1.15).

foreigners because they are expatriates. This expatriate mission is not in the process of vanishing, although those who execute it are changing. The missionary of the past who did everything is now being replaced by Christians of different professions. The great danger facing them is to regard their leaving of their own country as either an interesting experience or as a necessary evil and not as a *vocation*. This danger threatens the Westerners in particular because they can carry out their work without having to learn the language of the country to which they may go.

Partners

To the faith which is the first of all the qualities required in a missionary must also be added openness of spirit, curiosity, understanding and patience; all of these must stem from love; without this, his service outside his own country neither fulfils the conditions of a visit nor is it missionary.[1] There are still too many missionaries who work in foreign lands as if they were entirely on their own with no account to render except to themselves or to their far-distant agencies. Although their professional work may be useful, they fail in their mission which should consist in involving others in their action and in leading them towards a definite goal.

To render service, which is truly missionary, we must be open to the thoughts of our partner; we must attempt to see things from his point of view and according to his way of reasoning. This is the ABC of the love of one's neighbour; but unfortunately there are still many who are illiterate in this ABC, even among involved Christians. By putting ourselves in the place of our partner we come to understand, for example, that it is more difficult to receive than to give, so that 'he who gives, even generously, seldom receives the thanks that he believes he has deserved'.[2] To become a good partner we must expect nothing

[1] See above, pp. 81ff.
[2] *Conseils à l'intention des consultants internationaux*, United Nations 1965, p. 5.

of our partners and we must give evidence that we possess *imagination*. But imagination, like love, is a rare gift. Through lack of it, the missionary visitor is liable to think that certain current expressions have the same meaning for his partner as for himself, and this leads to misunderstandings which could have been avoided. Let us take nationalism as an example. To the Western Christian or humanist, nationalism is an evil to be fought against; for the African and the Asiatic it is a double benefit, first because it has enabled him to be set free from colonialism and to achieve independence, and secondly because it does unite very different tribes, who are often hostile to one another, within a given area. The Westerner needs to realize that the same word can have totally different meanings depending upon places and periods.[1] The idea of the picturesque is another subject of misunderstanding. In a developing society the picturesque is often evidence of a past which is being rejected; hence it is essential to distinguish between those elements of the past of which our partner is proud and those which he finds an embarrassment.

Men in rapidly developing countries have a foot in two cultures. They share through their work in the new technical and secular culture, but through their families they continue to be attached to the life of their tribe. This involves two systems of values, one for their work and one for their family life, and this is a constant source of conflict. The Western partner should show his understanding and his patience by restraining the judgment he is often tempted to pass on his partner who is compelled to live in two worlds at once.

The Westerner is often caught out by his partner's understanding of money, work, time and truth. He forgets that a new situation is created by the change from a tribal to a modern economy, just as much as by natural disasters or wars. Money is an abstraction in modern economics, and exchange, however precise it may be, is also symbolic and hence has an undefined value. It needs time to accord the same value to a sum of money as to a yoke of oxen. Moreover, the inflation which affects most

[1] K. H. Pfeffer, *Welt im Umbruch*, Gütersloh 1966, p. 181.

developing countries does not make the change from one economy to another any easier.

The Western concept of work is the result of a revolution that goes back to the beginning of the Christian era.[1] Manual work has ceased to be the exclusive province of the slave or of a particular class and has become an honourable pursuit which gives meaning to life. Moreover through its connexion with productivity, it provides for the neighbour the consumer goods which he lacks and at the same time is the source of personal comfort. The frugality and contentment that impress us so much when we come into contact with the rural populations of Africa and Asia are the outcome of a period of history when nature produced enough food for everyone, without the need for new techniques to obtain more. That age is finished. Everywhere populations are increasing and agriculture has to be transformed. What was previously an idyllic frugality and contentment is now rapidly becoming a lack of awareness, for if the peasant has to produce more than before, this is not in order to increase his profits (often this does not interest him) but in order that his children in the city may have something to eat. Until this is learned, we have to have much patience and especially imagination.

The Western understanding of time also produces much misunderstanding. To have a wristwatch does not mean that its owner is as yet able to divide time into hours, minutes and seconds and to organize himself upon this new basis. Both the observance of the sun and work in the countryside have habituated him to a less fragmented division of time.

The problem of truth has not been the subject of as careful studies as money, work and time. The Westerner attributes to the word a value different from that of the African or Asiatic. For them truth and non-truth are to be found at a level which is less external and more profound. It is not the correspondence of the words which concerns him, but the interior correspondence of sentiments. If we want to know what he thinks and then to

[1] See above, p. 10.

build upon his promises, we must not stumble over his words but must attempt to understand what is suggested by his words and attitudes. This way of communicating is only possible in an economic situation where time is not measured in seconds, and it will probably change with the introduction of the modern idea of time.[1] The idea of truth does not depend only upon the relation of words and feelings; it also rests upon the degree of confidence that one has in the other person. One who has reason to fear that his freedom may be abused in an attempt to dominate him will avoid the truth in order to stay free. What we often regard as falsehood is often only the last weapon of the weak against the strong. A tribe or a caste that has been oppressed by another for thousands of years develops defence reflexes that cannot be overcome in a day. The Westerner, especially if he is a missionary, would do well not to apply his oversimplified concept of truth to his partners; instead he should adapt himself to theirs and both take his time in speaking with them and try to gain their confidence.

This effort to understand is especially needed by the theologian, whether he devotes his whole life at work in Africa or Asia or travels there at his own expense for a limited period. This effort is indivisible from that love which is the driving force of the mission of God. Without understanding, wedded to knowledge and imagination, there is no love and service becomes only a mechanical performance of work.

In order to understand the often strange reactions to our

[1] Two examples: An Asiatic asks a European to take the chair at a special function on a certain date. The European, who knows that he will be elsewhere on that day, gives polite refusal, whereupon the Asiatic urges him to accept, even if he withdraws at a later stage. The European is shocked by this understanding of honesty; one does not agree to do something when one knows in advance that it is impossible. The Asiatic too is shocked by this understanding of honesty; in order to show that one appreciates the honour which is being offered, the invitation must be accepted even if one knows in advance that it must later be refused.

An Asiatic has his wristwatch stolen in Naples, and this is his first contact with Europe. In a similar case a European would have a violent reaction and would employ words that were scarcely flattering. The Asiatic, however, even avoids using the word 'stolen' and says: 'I have lost my watch because of Italian poverty.'

behaviour, we must attempt to understand ourselves.[1] Although
we have lost our sense of spiritual superiority, due to two world
wars, we have no doubts about our technical superiority. This
mixture of spiritual insecurity and technical competence, joined
to the pluralist and secular atmosphere in which we live, turns
us into sceptics. When we wax enthusiastic about so-called
primitive civilizations and praise their stability and refinements,
we do so with a certain detachment. This detachment is one of
the conditions for scientific experiment and one of the results of
the objectivity to which scientific advance has subjected us, as is
also scepticism in regard to traditional values; all this produces
a certain nihilism which can easily degenerate into cynicism,
even if we are Christians.

We only attach a relative importance to symbols, days, rites,
dogmas and even to the words of the bible. We are characterized
by a certain *radicalism*. We are satisfied with so little! For example,
we are satisfied with a Christ who is resurrected only in the
person of our neighbour or with a God with whom we have only
a nebulous relationship, somewhere within the depths of our
being. Our prayer is frequently no more than: 'I believe; help
my unbelief' (Mark 9.24).

We must admit that it is very difficult for our African, Asiatic
or South American partner to classify us: Christians? but they
go rarely to church. Christians? but they seldom read the bible
and their knowledge of it is largely lacking. Christians? but they
are horrified at the idea of praying in public and possibly of
prayer in general. Why do they come to us? No doubt with the
generous idea of communicating their techniques to us. Since
this is what we need, let us try to understand what they *do* – it
does not matter if we do not understand what they *are*.

Secularization has so affected us that we have become
indifferent to external signs of piety and love. Christ himself, of
course, was not a stranger to secularization; like the prophets,
he condemned purely external signs of piety and love, but he

[1] *Cf.* the section entitled 'The Fourth Man' in Hoekendijk, *op. cit.*,
pp. 45–59. The Fourth Man is post-Christian, post-ecclesiastical, post-
bourgeois, post-personal and post-religious.

did not demand that we should renounce signs, rather that we should ensure they truly signify that which they are supposed to signify. We should not forget that Christ prayed and gave instructions in prayer, and that he knew the scriptures and constantly referred his hearers to them; moreover he did institute the eucharist. Hence the Western Christian, away from his own country, should join in the worship of his partners, even if he does not understand the language; in this way he will prepare himself to join with them in the Lord's Supper. He should not be ashamed to reveal his Christian convictions, nor to pray, to read his bible and to study it with his brothers. Then his presence would not only be useful for communicating his technical know-how; it would be the opportunity for a mutual enrichment; it would be a *visit* which would transform his presence into a missionary presence.

Partners in Social Action

In addition to the general indications we have just provided, missionaries who are specialists in social action[1] must study the effects of development upon their own professions. The United Nations has published a number of studies which relate to this. A missionary agronomist should be familiar with the plans and projects of FAO and a doctor with those of OMS. They should also concern themselves with the spirit of their technique or art, for this spirit goes with the technique and creates problems for those who are learning it.[2]

The Christian technologist is caught between the extremes of Western rationalism and 'primitive' magic. The rationalist explanation of the physical and psychical phenomena that are at the basis of the techniques he is concerned to teach not only pushes back the frontiers of magic, it also tends to force them

---

[1] Teachers, doctors, nurses, economists, construction engineers, accountants, agronomists, technicians sent by a mission, a church or an organization for assistance having the specific aim of participating through their profession in the mission of the Church in the Third World.

[2] Pfeffer, *op. cit.*, pp. 128–36; Behrendt, *Soziale Strategie für Entwicklungsländer*, 1965, pp. 166–210.

into certain areas which are jealously reserved for them by their partners or pupils.[1] The rationalist explanation of the phenomena of existence, by its erosion of magical belief, also affects Christian faith, especially in those areas where it has only just liberated itself from magic. We are here faced with a problem that specialists in Christian action must resolve in co-operation with anthropologists and theologians.

Margaret Mead, the anthropologist, has questioned a number of ideas which derive from an outdated anthropology: 'each individual is dependent upon learning to become a full human being ... once this is recognized, it is clear that no aspect of any culture is irrelevant to the Christian ideal of man in community with his fellowmen.'[2] While we must recognize that the Christian message has been continually reinterpreted 'in terms of particular cultures and periods',[3] we must also affirm that 'a process of cultural transformation occurs as the message is received and transmitted in different cultures'.[4] Further, according to Margaret Mead, anthropology recognizes that Christianity is a culture that transcends local cultures, and is comparable in this respect to Buddhism or Islam or modern Communism, 'each of which also has developed a culture-transcending system which crosses the bounds of local cultures and can be learned by men of many different cultural backgrounds'.[5]

We have carefully avoided using the expression 'Christian culture' because of the confusion that easily arises between Western civilization and Christian culture. Yet it can be said

---

[1] See M. Field, *Search for Security in Ghana*, London 1960; K. H. Pfeffer, *op. cit.*, pp. 130f. *Réforme* (Paris, No. 1083) has the following quotation from the Catholic Archbishop of Zoa, Yaoundé: 'We Christians run the risk of exploiting the African's innate religious feeling without helping him to give a proper place to reason and the rational. It is necessary to liberate the scientific spirit from its primitive slavery.' Quotation from R. de Pury, who observes: 'Is it not remarkable that Christians of all traditions ultimately see that faith and science are mutually inclusive, whereas (Christian) faith and (natural) religion are mutually exclusive?' (*Des Antipodes*, Neuchâtel 1966, see p. 127, note 3, below.)

[2] *Man in Community*, ed. Egbert de Vries (Vol. IV of the 'Church and Society' Conference preparatory studies), London and New York 1966, p. 205.

[3] *ibid.*, p. 206.   [4] *ibid.*, p. 208.   [5] *loc. cit.*

that Western civilization has been the bearer of a certain
Christian culture, as long as we remember that there is no
necessary identification between what is borne and what bears.
The Christian technologist has to know that the message which
he carries, when he repeats and communicates his technical
activities in the perspective of his faith, transforms and re-
fashions the culture in which he is present. The surgeon's knife
does not suppress the magician, but it severely limits his
domain. In this very precise way he disrupts the magic circle
enclosing tribal life. He must perform this with love, and this
involves at least two things: he must explain or see that an
explanation is given of what is happening to the family, and he
must try and ensure that these people who have in this way been
opened to a new concept of life are cared for by those who have
received a revelation of the meaning and scope of this new life.

The excellent pamphlet issued by the United Nations and
entitled *Conseils à l'intention des consultants internationaux* in-
sists that to give advice is to teach and that to teach is largely
to explain. Often the technologist cannot explain because
having once understood the meaning of his actions he can
repeat them without difficulty and in fact needs to do so if he is
to make progress in his work. The unreflective and mechanical
communication of techniques is one of the great obstacles to
development in the Third World. If there is one sphere in which
the Christian technologist has a contribution to make, it is this
one. This involves explaining and looking for images in everyday life, for designs and models which can help people to understand the immediate and long-term goals of the technology that
is being communicated (e.g. the technique of maintaining in
good working-order some particular item of equipment such as
a car, a lorry or a machine) – all this is part of love for one's
neighbour. To say the contrary – here you are, do like this and
make the best of it – is both useless and brutal.

The technologist who devotes time to explaining what he is
doing will by this means be prevented from advancing too
quickly. The task of the missionary-technologist is not to make
as many things as possible on his own but to make some in

co-operation with his partners. Here is one of the great temp-
tations that face those missionaries who bear witness through
their work. It often seems to them that in order to preach by
their example they must accomplish as much work as possible;
they must give up free time and even kill themselves in their
work. There are of course occasions when the demands of one's
profession monopolize the entire person; doctors and nurses
know this only too well. Nevertheless, when excessive activity
becomes the rule, there is something amiss and a remedy must
be sought, for we not only have *to do* something for others, we
also have *to be* for others. The United Nations' pamphlet to
which we have just referred emphasizes the importance of
'cordial and unofficial talks' between us and our counterparts
in the Third World or between us and our students. It is in such
a conversation that we can explain the meaning of the work we
are doing together; we can learn to recognize our partners'
reactions; we can interest ourselves in their families, in the way
they are going, in the goals of which they have a glimpse for
themselves and their families; we can answer their questions
and we can communicate, often without being aware of it,
something of our faith and our hope.

Although the professional work of a Christian must take place
usually in terms of what we have called 'indirect compassion',
with the object of leading all the people in a region towards
development, it is also necessary to insist that this 'indirect
compassion' is to be accomplished in parallel with 'direct
compassion' which involves person to person contact. We therefore agree with Jacques Beaumont that 'the Christian function
in society is not primarily to find solutions to these problems
(hunger, migration, urbanization), but to reveal a way of life
which gives a basis for hope in a real community'.[1] This real
community requires person to person contact. That is why the
doctor, the teacher and the technologist *must* have time for these
contacts, either during or apart from their professional work.
If they do not have the time, *they must make it*. By dint of wish-
ing to do the best possible for the greatest number, we often

[1] *Vers une église pour les autres*, p. 162.

neglect persons and we reach the misleading result that many are helped a little, from the material point of view, while at the same time they are abandoned spiritually. The report of the conference on the serving role of the Church reminds us that we often eliminate persons in favour of a collectivity and that, with the help of the effective support the Church can give, we should 'direct our maximum effort towards developing a collectivity which is capable of care and compassion'.[1]

Partners in Proclamation

The Church and Society Conference has insisted upon the pastoral responsibility of the Church. The Church should help its members to relate their actions more closely to their Christian obedience, so that their decisions will reflect the care for and demands of Christ upon the world.[2] In this connexion, the preacher must make a great effort to understand what is involved in the decisions that the members of the Church have to take. He should not rest content with explaining the bible or teaching Christian doctrine. He needs to have a wide know-ledge of the human sciences (sociology, psychology, education) so that he can discuss to some purpose the problems that face the members of his Church and so that he can announce the Christian message in terms of these problems. More than lectures and books,[3] regular contact with the members of the

---

[1] *L'Eglise dans son rôle diaconal au sein de la société contemporaine*, p. 48.

[2] *World Conference on Church and Society*, p. 87.

[3] K. H. Pfeffer, *op. cit.*; R. F. Behrendt, *op. cit.*; R. Mehl, *Traité de sociologie du protestantisme*; the four preparatory volumes to the Church and Society Conference, 1966; H. D. Wendland, *Die Kirche in der revolutionaren Gesellschaft*, Gütersloh 1967; Christian Walther, *Theologie und Gesellschaft*, Zürich-Stuttgart 1967. See too H. R. Müller-Schwefe, *Die Lehre von der Verkündigung*, 1965, where the author discusses the problem of word and reality. Section 3, 'Proclamation and Reality', is particularly important, as is the critique of various methods of preaching – from Billy Graham to Rudolf Bultmann. The author argues that existentialist interpretation does not do justice to the word of God: 'It is up with the times; it has recognized that by interpreting reality, man realizes the world. But it runs out of words if it tries to describe this experience itself, that the world is interpreted by man. . . . What is bodily is not described. So modern interpretation does not

Church and his colleagues will provide him with the information he needs.[1]

The Inductive Method

The essential task of the preacher is to place his hearers within
the perspective of the mission of God in Jesus Christ for the
world and to make them missionaries by inviting them to let
themselves be integrated into the great current of love that
comes from God and is revealed in Jesus Christ, the final goal of
which is the communion of all in forgiveness and righteousness.
The foreign preacher, in conjunction with his partners, should
seek to discover the method appropriate to attain this goal.

In our view there should be no hesitation about the main
features of this method. It is largely that of the bible, viz.
induction. Induction is the action of leading someone towards
something (or someone). In the bible, induction refers mainly to
the great current of love which comes from God and advances
towards man. Our method is usually too deductive and not
sufficiently inductive.[2] We start off from certain theological
conclusions which the disciples of Jesus, and ourselves after
them, have reached and we forget that to become a Christian
each one has to follow the same road in his heart that leads from
Abraham to the Promised City, especially the road that goes
from Galilee to Emmaus by way of Golgotha. Every man has to
be confronted with the presence of the Son of Man, as were the
Galileans, and thus led to cry out in their turn, like Peter: 'You
are the Christ' (Mark 8.29), or like the centurion: 'Truly this
man was the Son of God!' (Mark 15.39).

---

really reach the realm of history, in which is involved the word that became
flesh' (*op. cit.*, pp. 111f.).

[1] In this connexion I wish to stress the importance of the dialogical
attitude as against the customary monological one: 'Communication is
interpreted to mean telling people what they ought to know. This is a
monological illusion. The preacher is so concerned about his message . . . that
he is blind to the real human needs of his hearers and to their search for
meaning' (J. G. Davies, *Dialogue with the World*, p. 35).

[2] J. A. T. Robinson, *The New Reformation?*, London and Philadelphia
1965, pp. 37, 51.

If to the Hindus we present Christ clothed in his divine attributes, they will see nothing unusual in him, because their religious tradition is full of divine descents to the earth where the gods, for a time, are clothed in human form. The incarnation of Vishnu or Krishna is an important element in Hinduism; hence an important distinction must be made between the biblical idea of incarnation and the Hindu concept of an avatar. This distinction is necessary, but the proclamation of the Gospel loses its cutting edge if it has to be accompanied by a series of distinctions which are difficult for the uninitiated to understand.[1] This may be avoided by presenting the Son of Man, as he presented himself to the Galileans, as a revolutionary being who turned their most cherished religious ideas upside down and set the neighbour in the centre of religious and moral concern. Then the Hindu is confronted by a new world into which he desires to penetrate and often does penetrate, though he is free to stop halfway like Ram Mohan Roy,[2] Gandhi and others who were pioneers in the Indian social movement.

The Church must without ceasing present the Son of Man to these men and women who are on the way, in the expectation that some day they will receive the grace to say with Peter: 'You are the Christ.' But the Church must take care not to be overhasty and not to offer ready-made formulae that are no more than dangerous shortcuts. The inductive method allows the preacher to make the distinctive message of the Gospel stand out so that it is received as the proclamation of a revolutionary order.

[1] See also H. R. Müller-Schwefe, 'Proclamation is a summons to the presence of the Lord. It is his will to be spoken of, so that we may believe in him. It is his will to interpret our present by his action, so that we can make steps into the future. It is not a question of teaching about interlinking themes in systematic theology, nor of moral exhortation nor of stirring the emotions. It is a question of letting Jesus Christ himself take life in the message and of his beginning to work there. Proclamation is not interpretation, but change. And this change takes place through the presence of the Lord in the Word' (*op. cit.*, p. 15. See also p. 218).

[2] 1778–1833, the first reformer of Hinduism and the editor of a selection from the Gospels entitled *An Appeal to the Christian Public in Defence of the Precepts of Jesus*. He explains in this why he has not reproduced the dogmatic passages and most of the miracles.

Beliefs

There are two questions that especially preoccupy the Western theologian working in Africa and Asia: these are the value to be attributed to the religious beliefs of the men amongst whom he is living and the way in which he should respond to their spiritual needs. The inductive method can help him considerably to deal with these problems. The Son of Man, as the Gospels describe him, fulfils the hopes of his contemporaries in a remarkable way: he revolutionizes their beliefs and gives their spiritual needs a new orientation.

In all ages theologians have tried to resolve the tension between traditional non-Christian beliefs and Christian belief by means of a very simple scheme of successive stages. So the non-Christian beliefs are presented as a preparatory stage leading to Christian faith which is itself their crown.[1] Today the attempt is being made to discover in non-Christian beliefs primary truths which though they may have to be toned down do not lose their importance. For example, an African teacher has noted that African religion, before the arrival of Christianity, knew of a God the Father and a God the Spirit. What Christianity brings therefore, according to him, is not something radically new but something complementary. Gandhi found his social teaching in the Bhagavadgita, although he admitted that it had been disclosed to him by the Sermon on the Mount and by the writings of Tolstoy and Ruskin.[2] J. V. Taylor has sought to show that African beliefs spring from a primal vision of the world in which spirit and matter, the sacred and the profane, form one whole.[3]

It has been established that all religious traditions, in one way or another, refer to a 'primal vision'. We should not, however, seek to contrast this with the spirit-matter dualism which is so much a feature of our Western civilization, because this would

---

[1] So the title of the classic work of J. N. Farquhar is *The Crown of Hinduism*.

[2] *Unto this Last* by Ruskin is an exposition of the parable of the labourers in the vineyard (Matt. 20.1–16); see M. K. Gandhi, *An Autobiography*, Ahmedabad 1927; 2nd impression 1959, p. 65.

[3] *The Primal Vision*, London and Philadelphia 1963.

be to forget that this dualism, to a certain extent, represents a necessary stage on the way that leads to perfect communion. The prophetic message which Jesus both took up and fulfilled is based upon an important distinction between God, man and nature and this is very different from the magical, naturalistic and cosmic synthesis adopted by the religions of the people surrounding Israel.[1] We must also beware of a too ready acceptance of the idea of the spiritual unity of pre-colonial cultures and we must not indulge in overhasty comparisons between African and biblical thought. There are some writers who draw a parallel between the African tradition which allows of no separation between the sacred and the profane and the biblical affirmation that there is no area of life outside the divine authority, and then they contrast these views with the Western matter-spirit dualism which has been imported recently into Africa.[2]

Careful examination of African and biblical thought does indeed reveal they are very different. African society does not separate the sacred from the profane because it regards everything as sacred. The Israelites encountered this concept among the Canaanites and they had to be detached from it by means of a painful process of desacralization in which the prophets played a major part. Nature was despoiled of its divine attributes and reduced to the role of a creature in subjection to God, as is man himself. It ceased to be regarded as an emanation of the divine which encloses man in a sacred magic circle of cosmic dimensions. In thus desacralizing nature, the message of the prophets, which in Jesus became the Gospel, liberated man from domination by magic, taboos, the stars – even the dead[3] – and allowed

[1] *Cf.* H. Berkhof, 'God in Nature and History', *Study Encounter*, I, No. 3, 1965.

[2] See A. Adegbola, 'From Tribalism to Nationhood' in *Christian Social Ethics in a Changing World*, ed. John C. Bennett, pp. 183–97.

[3] A particularly impressive example of the power of the dead over the living is offered by the feasts of the dead in Madagascar: 'The dead suck the living dry without contributing anything in return. The teams of workers who work for months at a stretch to make tombstones for the dead out of hewn granite cannot meanwhile build roads, plant vineyards, set up bean-poles, build factories, train as mechanics. But worst of all – where the

him to offer himself, body and soul, in the service of his Creator (Rom. 12.1).

It is being more and more recognized that at the origin of the present disturbances there lies a concept of man which is not in agreement with the traditional view. This 'hypothesis about man',[1] with which our world operates, has its roots in the biblical concept of man. It is a kind of humanism which can be described as Judaeo-Christian-Marxist. Roger Garaudy, the great theoretician of the French Communist Party, has said: 'That which gives meaning, beauty and value to life is for Marxists, as for Christians, the being able to give oneself without any limitation to that which the world can become

---

devilish business comes full circle – is the fact that even demography is subject to religious influence. People must bring up as many young as possible, so that there will be someone to care for them when they are dead. I say this quite emphatically: there is no hope and no future for the country unless the sense of its history is reversed, unless the church can see that the kingdom of God takes the place of the realm of the dead.

'Let "Bread for the Brethren", "Friends of the Third World" and "Co-opération" do what they can with all their technicians. They cannot be encouraged enough. But all their efforts will be in vain unless the Christians do their part as well (and I mean the native Christians, for they are the only ones who can do this): unless they disenchant their people. A cocaine addict is not cured without being (gradually) taken off the drug. Religion is opium for the people. Have we still not understood this? Ancestors as mystic beings are the opium for Madagascar. The dead and the gods are opium for all peoples. How can the Indians be nourished if the gods prohibit them from eating this and that? How can the Malagasy make adult decisions as long as they take refuge in the bosom of their dead, where everything has already been decided? No one there takes decisions . . . they let things run their course with the help of the *vasaha*. If "Coopération" and the mission were to continue to spare the Malagasy from *thinking ahead and making decisions* it would no doubt be better if they all went their way. This would provoke a fearful crisis. But at least people would then discover that there were others who were bearing the responsibility for the future of the people.

'I am quite aware that I am saying some very inappropriate things here. But I do not believe that a Christian should be afraid of being called a "blasphemer" in a world which is ossified to death when the Lord calls it to live; which clings to its gods when God offers it the resurrection of man; which shuts itself up in the beyond when God is opening the gates of the earth to it; which sinks into its graves when the Lord proclaims: "Whosoever believes on me shall never die"' (R. de Pury, *op. cit.*, pp. 49f.).

[1] This is a phrase used by J. Berque. See I. Hoechstetter, 'L'homme de la décolonisation', *Réforme*, 24 December 1966.

through our sacrifice.'[1] Although there are considerable differences between Judaism, Christianity and Marxism, it is undeniable that these three great streams of life do converge in a certain understanding of man, and that this concept is different from that to be found in those societies which have not undergone their influence.

Spiritual Needs

A missionary who has returned from Ghana has suggested that the most noticeable spiritual need of the inhabitants of that country is security.[2] Indeed this need is universal, and the preacher must take account of it and show how the Son of Man responds to it. His reply is in fact unexpected. Jesus provides 'security' by summoning men to adhere to him and to follow him. There is no other remedy. The healings that he performed in response to the crowd's distress were signs of a total healing, affecting life in its entirety. The sick person only receives this by following him, and there is no other way.

Unfortunately this undertaking to follow Jesus is often replaced by a purely spiritual attachment to his person. There is a mystical deviation in Christianity which results in a false security; religious life becomes a duet between the soul that has been saved and the mystical Lamb. This duet can be very beautiful and we must acknowledge the way in which it has inspired some splendid Baroque music. The Gospel is not against the mystic; he even has a special place (Mark 14.3–9; John 12.1–8). But the Gospel is opposed to allowing this to become a substitute for that involvement in the world to which the Master calls his disciples. Mysticism is a stage; one can indeed say that it is the Christian's Sunday compared with his week, when he must take up again the road as he follows his tireless Master (Matt. 8.18–22).

On the road, following his Master, the Christian meets his

---

[1] *Time Magazine* (Atlantic Edition), 30 December 1966. See also 'Dialogue with R. Garaudy', *La Vie Protestante*, 7 April 1967.

[2] See the remarkable study by M. Field, *Search for Security in Ghana*.

neighbour. This is the complete antithesis of that security which he believes that he needs and which induces him to surround himself with defences and, as it were, trace a magic circle around himself. It is possible to hold, in the light of the Gospel, that Jesus has come to replace this feeble magic circle with the all-powerful circle of his person. In other words, Jesus comes to set man free from himself. He provides him with 'security' not by surrounding him with a circle, but by sending him to his neighbour[1] whom he has to provide with security by making him a pioneer of the Kingdom that is to come.

Discouragement

One of a preacher's essential tasks is to fight against discouragement. Westerners are profoundly disillusioned after two world wars, the hydrogen bomb and the Vietnam war which have dealt a severe blow to the idea of progress by means of democracy and compulsory education. The difficulties attendant upon decolonization have also led an increasing number of people in the Third World to a similar state of disillusionment. While Westerners, somewhat disabused of their hopes in terms of their immense development, are repeating in a mechanical fashion their same technological activities and even improving upon them, the inhabitants of the Third World find themselves on the edge of an abyss and are tempted either to give up everything or to turn everything upside down by having recourse to an anti-human and cynical reign of terror.[2] At its extremes this despair turns into a nihilism of either violence or of spirit. The latter is manifested by the effort to achieve a disengagement from spiritual concerns.[3] This is being effected by philosophical and religious movements which have parallels in all the religions including Christianity. The world is renounced. Phenomena are disregarded in favour of a search for essence. Action appears meaningless and of no use; history is treated as a parenthesis.

---

[1] 'Go, and do likewise' (Luke 10.37).
[2] See K. H. Pfeffer, *op. cit.*, pp. 209–18.
[3] It is very well illustrated by M. West's novel, *The Ambassador*.

'Everything is in everything; there is nothing new.' It is with this philosophy that many are approaching the world, men, themselves and even the bible. The books of Job, Ecclesiastes and the Apocalypse seem to support this position.

The preacher has the difficult task of lifting these 'drooping hands' and strengthening these 'weak knees' (Heb. 12.12). When Christian hope transcends present experience in the world and is directed towards a fulfilment that is the object of faith it readily assumes a metaphysical aspect. This is not an aspect that should be to the fore, rather it should be recognized that Christian hope relates to the present. We have to make the effort to disclose here and now the definite promises of final fulfilment; we have to point to the good wheat in the midst of the chaff; we have to affirm what has changed in life, although taken as a whole it may appear not to have altered. The certainty of a consummation does not allow us to despise small beginnings: 'for whoever has despised the day of small things?' (Zech. 4.10).

When Jesus says, 'Today has salvation come to this house' (Luke 19.9), he means that something very concrete has happened. Zacchaeus has been effectively set free from corruption and this change in his life has probably had repercussions well beyond his own household.

Spiritual nihilism has been stimulated by the disillusionment that has arisen from the blocking of men's efforts to improve their condition and it finds support in the inevitable presence of suffering and death in the world. The bible only partly raises the veil that covers this mystery; however it does indicate that suffering and death are not the inevitable accompaniment of birth and life, which is the belief of the adherents of those religions that are based upon the rhythm of nature and whose fertility rites reach great heights of philosophical and mystical development.[1] Suffering and death, according to the bible, are

[1] See Jürgen Moltmann, *Theology of Hope*, 1967, p. 24: 'The despairing surrender of hope does not even need to have a desperate appearance. It can also be the mere tacit absence of meaning, prospects, future and purpose. It can wear the face of smiling resignation: *bonjour tristesse!* All that remains is a certain smile on the part of those who have tried out the full range of

the result of the wrong use man has made of the extraordinary freedom accorded to him by the Creator; since they result from disobedience, they can be overcome by obedience. It was by his perfect obedience that the Servant of Yahweh took upon himself suffering and death and opened the way to the great revolution, the ultimate end of which is perfect communion from which suffering and death are for ever banished.

This is why true encouragement does not consist in saying: Be patient; wait; the day will come when things will be better. Instead true encouragement says: Are you discouraged? are you suffering? You are not alone. Your suffering is shared. Many suffer like you and perhaps some are suffering *for* you. Do not suffer passively any longer; suffer actively. Believe that suffering is the means used by God to advance his Kingdom. Know that every act of suffering accepted in obedience brings you nearer, you and humanity, to the goal towards which we are on the march.

The Christian's mission is to be present actively for others. This mission of love often comes up against refusal, and of all sufferings that is the hardest. But it is the instrument that can change refusal into a joyful acceptance which sets constructive forces free.

That which counts above all is the obedience of faith. Jesus proclaims it by inviting the men of his day to follow him. The obedience of faith, with all the suffering that that involves,[1] draws the Christian into the great movement of love that bears

---

their possibilities and found nothing in them that could give cause for hope. . . . But where hope does not find its way to the source of new, unknown possibilities, there the trifling, ironical play with the existing possibilities ends in boredom, or in outbreaks of absurdity.'

[1] "Obedience" is the attitude which God expects from man, from Israel and from the righteous man in Israel, according to the Old Testament and Jewish witnesses. Not only is the word used in the New Testament and its environment "quite predominantly of obedience to the deity and his commandments" (Bauer, *Wörterbuch*, Berlin 1958); above all, it is witnessed always as the characteristic of the work of Jesus (Heb. 5.8 and earlier, Rom. 5.19).' E. Schweizer, *Erniedrigung und Erhöhung bei Jesus und seinen Nachfolgern*, Zürich 1962, p. 174 (not in the English edition). See also *ibid.*, 'Die Nachfolge Jesu in der Gemeinde', pp. 126–44.

the Creator towards his creatures and it makes them the bearers of hope.

This obedience is only possible because there is also forgiveness. Only the proclamation of forgiveness, which allows new beginnings, can lift up the drooping hands and strengthen the weak knees (Heb. 12.12). It alone can give courage to the discouraged; it alone can enable one to face one's self and accept one's mistakes and faults. Forgiveness starts off the movement of love which our disobedience is always compromising, even within the community of believers. It alone provides a sound basis for hope in the midst of the situations of despair. It alone enables men to go forward and truly progress.

Appendices

1 The Gospel, Religions and Cultures

R. de Pury:

To be on good terms with one's surroundings and by so doing to preserve social etiquette is as it were the indisputable order of the day. A breach with the family by keeping away from the family tomb causes real trouble. In this society, Christianity spread like lightning and became entangled with existing religious feelings. This was followed by a standstill. The Merina becomes a Christian all too easily and is therefore never a real Christian. Among the Betsileos and the Merinas (the most strongly Christianized families on the island), Christianity makes no progress. People waver to and fro. They maintain their innate relativism. As Father Ralibera put it: 'The danger for the Church is Malagasy religiosity. In the end, the so-called stages of preparation are simply hindrances.' It is unusual to hear a Roman Catholic priest make a statement so reminiscent of Kierkegaard and Luther, or to cast doubt on the much-vaunted 'stepping-stone theology' ('*théologie des pierres d'attente*') which has so recently dominated the Vatican Council's declaration on religion. It is all the more remarkable, as Father Ralibera had returned from Europe steeped in this theology, and as a result of mission work among the people of his area and in view of the conditions of Malagasy life came to discover how illusory it was. Religion does not 'bind' men to God; its effect is rather to keep them away. It does not bring men nearer to the God of Abraham, but removes them from him (Roland de Pury, *Des Antipodes*, Neuchâtel 1966, pp. 68f.).

On this theme, see also Roger Mehl, *Traité de sociologie du protestantisme*, Neuchâtel-Paris 1966, pp. 147ff. In this chapter on the sociology of missions, Mehl takes up some quite daring statements from *Décolonisation et Mission*, which he makes more profound and detailed. On the unavoidable changes brought about by the preaching of the Gospel, Mehl writes:

In a general way it can be said that the Christian mission has not always been very concerned about the social changes it has introduced by its own evangelistic action amongst people in other countries. But it is also necessary to point out why it has not been concerned. *The Christianity which engaged in missionary action, beginning in the eighteenth century, was the Christianity of a society which had already been profoundly secularized, i.e. a society in which the Churches had become differentiated societies in relation to world society.* They did indeed exercise a wide influence upon that society, but the main structures of that society were already on the way to laicization; it was already possible to live in the society without being a Christian. Confessional adherence had either become a private matter or was fast becoming one. The Pietistic colouring of many of these missionary societies was in fact a reflection of this situation, which involved a certain dichotomy – on the one hand existence in a world society and on the other a more or less free adherence to a Church. The whole technological, economic, political and social evolution took place, especially in the nineteenth century, apart from the influence of the Church. There was a common morality, no doubt permeated with Christianity but distinct from it. It was in this situation that the Christian missions thought out their apostolic action. They went across the seas to preach the Gospel, to convert souls to the Lord. They were unable to calculate the sociological effects of their action (pp. 156f., my italics).

Mehl makes an apt criticism of a certain 'integrationist' missiology:

There can be no doubt that reforms are needed and that the Christian Church must try to forward them. This is not a question of raising doubts about the well-based spirituality of its demands. But it does need to realize that many of these are in danger of creating a social vacuum and a breaking up of the structures of social care without the possibility of a new order being substituted.

The problem is all the more serious because these structures and the traditions that support them are not being questioned by missionary action alone, which to a certain degree can integrate those who are converted into parochial communities, rather *the decisive clash arises out of the encounter of these civilizations with economic needs.* The circulation of goods will surpass the circulation of people. Economic changes will effect not only a change in the techniques of production but also in the social structures themselves. *In view of the speed and brutality of these changes, the social vacuum could be terrifying. This can already be seen in the shanty towns that have sprung up around many great conurbations*; here, more or less penned up, are many individuals who have come from very different backgrounds; they have escaped from all traditional direction and from the healthy disciplines of their tribes; they no longer have any experience of withdrawal for the purpose of initiation and they are incapable of integrating themselves into the new society because they constitute a kind of subproletariat. The only refuge for these people lies in sexual licence, alcoholism and sometimes in a political party (pp. 159f., my italics).

Mehl goes on to argue with E. Benz:

It must be acknowledged that this insertion of Christianity into civilizations that have been formed by paganism is a very difficult task. It is not to be achieved simply by adopting a few indigenous customs, traditions or institutions. It requires a very definite theological effort to avoid a kind of doctrinal syncretism which favours this adoption of institutions and customs. It requires a kind of Christian baptism of these factors.

Mehl then quotes Ernst Benz:

The most important task to be accomplished in India, in order that Christianity may be manifested in a proper manner, is the creation of a positive link between the Gospel message and the spiritual content of the great traditions that are native to India, just as the early Church established a link between the Gospel and Greek philosophy. It is necessary, therefore, especially for the theology of the younger Churches, to discover the positive link between the evolution of the religious conscience in the great non-Christian Asiatic religions and the Christian message – in other words, we must seek to understand the religious evolution of the great Asiatic faiths, which are non-Christian, as a soteriological event, as an element in the history of salvation (Benz: 'Manilal Parekh, Le Gandhi chrétien', *Le monde non-chrétien*, Nos. 55–6, 1960).

Mehl quotes this text in order to show

that the problem is far from being a simple one. A *civilization is homogeneous. It is difficult to extract certain elements* (institutions, customs) *and to unite them within a spirituality whose direction is entirely different.* There is a risk that these elements will carry with them something of their original spirituality and that in this way the road to syncretism may be opened. Indeed not even Ernst Benz is free from this since he is prepared to regard the great Asiatic faiths as belonging to the history of salvation (pp. 161ff., my italics).

2 Church and World

Roger Mehl:

It is a sociological fact worthy of note that the thought of the Churches, especially of the Protestant ones, is at present very much dominated by the theme of *presence in the world*. This theme lies at the basis of many theological works; it is being examined at every cultural level; it is to be found on the agenda of synods, ecclesiastical assemblies and even upon that of the Vatican Council. This theme of presence in the world has even opened up new aspects of theological research which would have surprised the classic theologians: *theology of the world, of work, of culture, of leisure.* The multiplication of these discussions and studies, which often content themselves with raising problems, shows that the Churches have entered into a new age in which they have to rediscover their place in society, simply because that place has not been prepared for them in advance and societies are organizing themselves without reference to such a place. This thinking is not only at the academic level. It is finding its outlet in all kinds of innovation and institutions. Many of these have an educational reference: the increase in lay academies shows that the Churches are aware of the need for a long period of preparation before they can undertake their new task or rather before they can assume new forms of presence in the world.

Although the problem of the Church's preaching is primarily a theological one and although its content is determined by its object, i.e. the biblical revelation, the direction of this preaching and the *hic et nunc* emphasis upon one or other of its elements must be determined by the sociological context of the preaching. *Hence the theme of presence in the world, i.e. of the actualization of the preaching, draws the attention of pastors, laity and ecclesiastical gatherings at the present day.* To define this actualization, especially in those Churches, like the Reformed, that insist strongly on the responsibility of the faithful in society, a number of sociological concerns have to be taken into account: social background, professional interests, age and sex. But there is one sociological problem in particular which has dominated thinking over the past decades and that is the development of the technological character of world civilization. For a civilization produces its own values and its own vision of the world. As Max Weber has often emphasized, the vision of the world that emerges from an essentially technological and non-magical society is a disenchanted vision. Both the world and existence are deprived of their mystery. The major part of human effort is directed to the resolution of problems which are problems of the adaptation of means to ends, and these ends then become means to further ends and so on. It is as if the ends were being absorbed or reabsorbed by the means. . . . *If it is true that the Gospel gives life and hope, how can the Churches respond to this boredom experienced by disenchanted souls?* We cannot give an answer to this question, but we can note, as a sociological fact, that Protestantism, having devoted decades to moralizing preaching, has, some thirty years ago, rediscovered the importance of the proclamation of the Kingdom, first as the archetype of social justice (the Christian Social Movement, Stockholm 1925), and then as an eschatological reality, as a source of hope. Those theological studies that give much weight to eschatology are innumerable and they have led to a renewal of preaching. Obviously this fact can be interpreted in diverse ways: faced with the disenchantment of the world, the Church can find in this hope a kind of alibi or evasion, so renewing the experience of many sects, *or the hope of the last things is indeed conceived as the spiritual reality that can give a value and a new flavour to daily life in affluent and secure societies. In this latter case, eschatology does not become the grounds for a mythical evasion but encourages the development of ethics.* At least that would appear to be the road traversed so far by Protestantism. Whether one looks at the theology of Barth or at that of Bultmann, each very different in their understanding of eschatology, both establish a link between eschatological faith and ethics. We *must emphasize the coincidence of these two phenomena: the disenchanted view of the world produced by technological and industrial societies on the one hand, and the rediscovery and re-evaluation of the eschatological dimensions of the Gospel on the other.* It is in this coincidence that the Church expresses its will to be present to the world. It is by attempting to respond to the evils that affect human existence, because of social changes, that the Church, in a secularized society that does not anticipate anything other than a marginal place for it or indeed ignores it entirely, will obtain a new social function, which is much less linked than in the past to the fulfilment of certain social rites which were held to be indispensable (Roger Mehl, *op. cit.*, pp. 276f., 278f., my italics).

3 Secularization

Hermann Lübbe quotes the American sociologist Howard Becker from the *Kölner Vierteljahrhefte für Soziologie*, 1932 (*Sekularisierung, Geschichte eines ideen politischen Begriffs*, Freiburg-München, 1965, p. 60). Howard Becker would like to introduce this word 'secularization' as the name of a social process, conceived in 'ideal-typical' terms, as a movement of society from the 'closed sacred society' to the 'open worldly society'. Contemporary and synchronous examples of these two societies are 'for the former . . . the clan structure which characterizes mainland China, and for the latter certain manifestations in cosmopolitan New York'. Lübbe also points out that in the USA secularism has never been the fighting programme of a social group as happened on the continent of Europe. In the USA the division of State and Church does not represent 'irreligion, weakness in the life of faith, but rather its strength and power in society, whose citizens founded their state in freedom from the church to guarantee the church at any time freedom in society' (*op. cit.*, pp. 131f.). In German-speaking theological usage secularization represented the process of man's emancipation, not only from the Church, but from God as well; the verdict on it thus had to be negative. Lübbe demonstrates that this negative verdict in Germany after the Second World War lasted until the currency reform: 'the crisis-experience of the collapse was followed by the experience of an unsuspected development of the powers of a fully secularized industrial society in terms of economics, technology and science. The secular process achieved by these forces seemed irresistible, and the prospects were by no means only threatening ones. Did it not offer the possibility for man to guarantee the material conditions of his existence for the first time in history? *Why should it not be possible to integrate this process in the economy of salvation, even if dialectically there was always the danger of being diverted in the opposite direction by the powers of evil?* . . . Such impressive considerations ultimately had to have consequences for the theological criticism of secularization' (*op. cit.*, p. 118, my italics). Lübbe then goes on to evaluate Friedrich Gogarten's *Verhängnis und Hoffnung der Neuzeit, die Säkularisierung als theologisches Problem*, Stuttgart 1953.

Let us now turn to Gogarten. Gogarten defines secularization as 'the transference of Christian insights and experiences from the realm of revelation and faith to that of universal human reason and at the same time the transformation of the reality of God known and experienced in them into that of man' (*op. cit.*, p. 9). Gogarten has understood that it is impossible to 'turn back the tide of secularization', because it is clear 'on the basis of the evidence of studies of human thought' that secularization 'is an effect of Christian faith' (*op. cit.*, pp. 9f.). He therefore investigates the connexion between faith and secularization and is led in the process of his investigation to make the important distinction between secularization and secularism. For him, secularism is the 'degeneration of secularization' (*op. cit.*, pp. 143f.). Either secularism appears as a saving doctrine or an ideology which differentiates itself from the truly secular 'investigation of the whole on an agnostic basis' (*op. cit.*, p. 147), and 'anticipates the historical decisions which fall to be made on different occasions in a once-for-all, all-embracing act' (*ibid.*); in other words, it provides an ideological basis; or, questions which concern the whole are left on one side, 'as they cannot be answered' (*op. cit.*, p. 143), and there arises 'the secularism which latently or openly declares any question which goes beyond what is merely visible and tangible to be useless and senseless. This kind of secularism has recently been called nihilism' (*ibid.*).

4 Excursus on J. Moltmann's *Theology of Hope*

The position of Jürgen Moltmann in his *Theology of Hope*, 1967, can be expressed in the following sentence: 'In expounding the promises in the Christ event in terms of latency and tendency, we discovered a historic process of mediation between subject and object, which allows us neither to assign the future of Christ to a place within some system of world history and of the history of salvation, and thereby make this event relative to something that is foreign to it, acquired from other experiences and imposed upon it from without, nor yet to reflect the future of Christ into the existentialistic futurity of man' (*op. cit.*, p. 225). Moltmann dissociates himself from late federal theology and the early pietistic theology of history which sets out 'to construe revelation in historic terms and see the history of the world as revelation', thus making possible a 'progressive' view of revelation: 'The revelation in Christ is thus placed under the head of a history of revelation, whose progressiveness is expressed in the idea of the developing of salvation stage by stage according to a previously fixed plan of salvation. This theology of the "plan" of saving history has many striking parallels with the scientific deism of the seventeenth and eighteenth centuries and is in every sense a religious product of the Enlightenment' (*op. cit.*, pp. 69f.). What Moltmann appreciates in this theology is the question 'of the future and goal which the Christian revelation contains' (*op. cit.*, p. 72). But he criticizes its attempt 'to discover the eschatological progressiveness of salvation history not from the cross and the resurrection, but from other "signs of the times"' (*ibid.*), such as the corruption of the Church, the decay of the world, etc. This criticism is justified. But whether Moltmann has succeeded in taking forward successfully the important question of 'the inward tendency and eschatological outlook which the divine revelation in history has towards the future' is another matter. We agree with Moltmann in his dissatisfaction with an eschatology which 'reflects the future of Christ into the existentialistic futurity of man' (*op. cit.*, p. 225). We also agree with him that the Kingdom of God is not to be spiritualized and made into an other-worldly entity, but that its this-worldly character is to be stressed (see *op. cit.*, p. 222). But we are not quite satisfied with the way in which this is to be done.

The difficulty is the this-worldliness of the conflict and the contrast with 'a godless and god-forsaken world'.

Is conflict and opposition all that can be said about the historical world (which in terms of latency and tendency is also a historical revelation of God)? In connexion with the 'Future of Righteousness', Moltmann writes: 'If in the justification of the sinner God attains to his rights, then this justification is the beginning and foreshadowing of his sole lordship. The divine righteousness which is latent in the event of Christ has an inner trend towards a totality of new being. The man who is justified follows this trend in bodily obedience. His struggle for obedience and his suffering under the godlessness of the world have their goal in the future of the righteousness of the whole. Thus this struggle is a fragment of, and a prelude to, the coming divine righteousness, for it already gives God his due, and in it already God attains to his rights over his world' (*op. cit.*, p. 207). Our impression is that Moltmann does not maintain the conflict here, but concedes that from this conflict grow fruits which are concrete, *real* indications of the totality of the new being. That must, however, mean that the new already begins in the midst of the old (fragments), not only in *conflict* with the old, but even *by shaping* the old in the direction of the new tendency. The form of the world, even the form of the world which in fragments is being given a new shape by Christians' struggle for obedience (I Cor. 7.31), is passing away. But the tendency remains. We are not to conceive of this tendency along the lines of ancient philosophy as a 'substance', but in biblical terms, as life. It is new life in the midst of the old. The section on 'The Future of Life' (*op. cit.*, pp. 208–16) is probably the most illuminating concerning Moltmann's position. He sees quite rightly that for the Old Testament, 'the "vacuum" caused by the absence of religious ideas and hopes against death . . . is only filled by a hope which makes possible a whole-hearted, unrestricted and unreserved assent to life, to the body and to the world, and which extends beyond death' (*op. cit.*, p. 210). Moltmann does not show clearly what difference the death and resurrection of Christ makes in this respect. The ominous ancient idea of redemption of corporeality is taken over without the necessary changes being made in the light of the Old Testament and the Christ event: 'This corporeality, for the redemption of which the man of hope waits because it has not yet taken place, is the existential starting-point for the university that marks the Christian hope and for the as yet undetermined character of what is hoped for' (*op. cit.*, p. 214). This 'existential starting-point', whose universality cannot be denied, is not, however, a starting-point for the universality of the *Christian hope*. For Christian hope does not primarily relate to the redemption of corporeality (as the ancient religions and still today, in the East), but to the fulfilment of the life which is expressed in corporeality in judgment and grace, to the 'wholehearted, unrestricted and unreserved assent to life, to the body and to the world' (see *op. cit.*, p. 191). This is our understanding of the promise in the death and resurrection of Jesus Christ.

Whether this fulfilment presupposes a *creatio ex nihilo* (cf. pp. 210, 221 and 226) is highly doubtful. The introduction of this concept does not clarify anything. It is not the *creatio ex nihilo* that is important, but the gracious act of God (*progressio gratiae*, p. 215). And this gracious act always also includes judgment. But judgment does not create right by destroying *everything* and making *all* things new, but by cleansing, purifying, *differentiating*. This differentiating is not to be derived immediately from the analogy of the death and resurrection of Christ, but from the analogy of baptism which promises and bestows new life upon men in the death and resurrection of Christ. The identity of the person baptized is maintained through his baptism. What happens to him is cleansing and *purification*. The category of judgment or purification is much more important for our understanding of the future of Christ, the new life and the new world than that of *creatio ex nihilo*. We can only speak of 'progressive revelation' or 'realized eschatology' in connexion with the grace of judgment. Only in the light of this differentiation can the following statement by Moltmann be understood: 'It is the inner necessity of the Christ event itself, the tendency of which is finally to bring out in all things *the eternal life latent in him and the justice of God latent in him*' (*op. cit.*, p. 216, my italics).

In the section 'Summary and Review' (*op. cit.*, pp. 224–9), Moltmann defines eschatology as 'speaking of Christ and his future' in 'the language of promises'. History is thus the 'reality instituted by promise' (*op. cit.*, p. 224). The Christian community is sent in this reality, opened up through the promise, to all nations. The *promissio* leads to *missio*. But in what does this mission consist? In 'the hunger for divine right in the godless world', in 'the struggle for public, bodily obedience' (*op. cit.*, p. 225). Moltmann can also say: 'The mission on which the man of hope is sent . . . pursues the direction of the tendency of God's own action . . .' (*op. cit.*, p. 227). But that also means that the revelation does not acquire 'the character of the progressive' through its entry into human history, but itself bestows this character on human history. The tendency and intention of God is that of a *progressio*, and this tendency and intention might, as we have attempted to show in the first part of this study, appear clearly within human history for the believer. There is a 'Populorum Progressio' (Papal Encyclical of Pope Paul VI of 28 March 1967) only because there is a *spiritus sancti progressio*. There is a progress of the nations only because there is a progress of the spirit towards its sacred goal. Unfortunately this view does not appear in the fundamental thought of the encyclical, but rather the ancient understanding of God, as the first truth and the supreme good (*Populorum Progressio*, 16: in *World Poverty and British Responsibility*, London 1967, p. 86). As far as Moltmann is concerned, he hesitates to draw the final conclusions from this view because for him only radical new creation, *creatio ex nihilo*, can follow from death and resurrection. It follows from this that the tendency and intention of God and the mission of the community that is to be derived from it, which is witnessed to by public and bodily obedience in the world and in human history on the part of the believers, does no more than raise hopes and bear the character of rebellion. True, the reality 'given now and experienced now' of the presence of Christ is not radically (*totaliter*) different from the reality of his future or parousia, but its effect in the present is that of a 'future that is really outstanding', achieved by 'awaking hopes and establishing resistance' (*op. cit.*, p. 227). Do we not have here that all too narrow eschatology which, as Karl Barth says, sets the demons free in 'a kingdom on the left hand of uncontrolled and undisciplined reality'? Is human history and the world for Moltmann simply 'a realm of hopelessness', because it is voided of 'pure hope for the last things' and the 'positive signs' of these last things are completely lacking? (K. Barth, *Church Dogmatics*, IV 3, 2, pp. 902-42). If we can only say about the next to last things that they awaken hopes and are the occasion for resistance in the obedience of faith, then no social, economic or political expression of this obedience is possible even in the next to last things as a positive sign of the last things, as 'an actual foretaste of God's consummating purposes' (Paul Lehmann, *Ethics in a Christian Context*, p. 70). Theology and society break apart. We are landed in the position of Jaques Ellul. Karl Barth, Roger Mehl, Arthur Rich, Paul Lehmann and Christian Walther have another theological

view which makes it possible for them to speak not only of the
awakening of hopes and the resistance of faith but also of the
making concrete of hopes, of positive fruits of Christian obedience
in present society, whose reality as next-to-last can no more be
separated *totaliter* from the last reality than the presence of Christ
from his future. Only in this way, we feel, can hope be something
other than a comfort for the future; only in this way can the this-
worldliness of the kingdom of God be asserted over against a
spiritualization of it.

Select Bibliography

P. ABRECHT, *The Churches and Rapid Social Change*, SCM Press and Doubleday & Co., London and New York 1961

R. F. BEHRENDT, *Soziale Strategie für Entwicklungsländer*, S. Fischer Verlag, Frankfurt 1965

J. C. BENNETT (Ed.), *Christian Social Ethics in a Changing World*, SCM Press and Association Press, London and New York 1966

E. BENZ, *Asiatische Begegnungen*, Eugen Diederichs Verlag, Düsseldorf-Cologne 1963

H. BERKHOF, 'God in Nature and History', *Study Encounter*, I, 3, WCC, Geneva 1965

W. BIEDER, 'Gottes Sending und der missionarische Auftrag der Kirche nach Matthaus, Lukas, Paulus und Johannes', *Theol. Studien*, 82, Zürich 1964

A. BIELER, *Calvin, prophète de l'ère industrielle, Débats*, 3, Labor et Fides, Geneva 1964

F. BLANKE, *Missionsprobleme des Mittelalters und der Neuzeit*, Zwingli Verlag, Zürich-Stuttgart 1966

J. BLAUW, *Gottes Werk in dieser Welt*, Chr. Kaiser Verlag, Munich 1961

E. BLUM, *Die Mission der Reformierten Schweiz*, Basileia Verlag, Basel 1965

M. Boss, *Indienfahrt eines Psychiaters*, Neske, Pfullingen 1969

P. VAN BUREN, *The Secular Meaning of the Gospel*, SCM Press and the Macmillan Company, London and New York 1963

H. BURKLE, *Dialog mit dem Osten*, Evangelisches Verlagswerk, Stuttgart 1965

G. CASALIS, W. J. HOLLENWEGER and P. KELLER (Eds.), *Vers une église pour les autres*, Labor et Fides, Geneva 1966

H. Cox, *The Secular City*, SCM Press and the Macmillan Company, London and New York 1965

G. CRESPY, *De la science à la théologie, Cahiers théologiques*, 54, Delachaux et Niestlé, Neuchâtel-Paris 1965

J. G. DAVIES, *Worship and Mission*, SCM Press and Association Press, London and New York 1966

J. G. DAVIES, *Dialogue with the World*, SCM Press, London 1967
— *Diakonie als oekumenische Aufgabe II. Die Verantwortung der Kirche in der Sozialarbeit*, Christlicher Zeitschriften-Verlag, Berlin 1962
— *Eglise et Guérison*, WCC, Geneva 1965
J. ELLUL, *Fausse présence au monde moderne*, Les Bergers et les Mages, Paris 1963
C.-H. FAVROD, *La faim des loups*, Editions de la Baconnière, Neuchâtel 1961
M. FIELD, *Search for Security in Ghana*, Faber & Faber, London 1960
M. K. GANDHI, *An Autobiography*, Navajivan Publishing House, Ahmedabad, 2nd ed. 1959
N. GOODALL, *Christian Missions and Social Ferment*, Epworth Press, London 1964
F. HAHN, *Mission in the New Testament*, SBT 47, SCM Press and Alec R. Allenson, London and Illinois 1965
P. HAZARD, *La crise de la conscience européene 1680–1715*, Fayard, Paris 1961
E. HEIMANN, *Du und die andern*, Paul Haupt, Berne 1965
A. H. VAN DEN HEUVEL, *The Humiliation of the Church*, SCM Press and Westminster Press, London and Philadelphia 1967
J. C. HOEKENDIJK, *The Church Inside Out*, SCM Press and Westminster Press, London and Philadelphia 1967
M. HOLLIS, *Paternalism and the Church*, OUP, London and New York 1962
L. J. KRAMER, *Man amid Change in World Affairs*, Friendship Press, New York 1964
R. A. LAMBOURNE, *Community, Church and Healing*, Darton, Longman and Todd, London 1963
A. T. VAN LEEUWEN, *Christianity in World History*, Edinburgh House Press, London 1964
P. LEHMANN, *Ethics in a Christian Context*, SCM Press and Harper & Row, London and New York 1963
M. LINZ, *Anwalt der Welt*, Kreuz Verlag, Stuttgart-Berlin 1964
H. J. MARGULL (Ed.), *Mission als Strukturprinzip*, WCC, Geneva 1965
R. MEHL, *Décolonisation et missions protestants*, Société des Missions Evangeliques, Paris 1964
— *Traité de sociologie du protestantisme*, Delachaux et Niestlé, Neuchâtel 1966
H. MEYER, *Wir lieben Indien*, MBK. Verlag, Salzuflen 1963

K. H. MISKOTTE, *When the Gods are Silent*, Collins and Harper & Row, London and New York 1967

J. MOLTMANN, *Theology of Hope*, SCM Press and Harper & Row, London and New York 1967

B. MOREL, *Cybernétique et éthique chrétienne*, Les cahiers protestants, 2, Lausanne 1966

N.-P. MORITZEN, *Die Kirche als Mission*, Das Gespräch, 66, Jugenddienst Verlag, Wuppertal-Barmen 1966

M. NASH, *Christians – World Citizens*, Edinburgh House Press, London 1965

S. NEILL, *Creative Tension*, Edinburgh House Press, London 1959

— *Colonialism and Christian Missions*, Lutterworth Press and McGraw-Hill Book Co., London and New York 1966

L. NEWBIGIN, *A Faith for this One World?*, SCM Press and Harper & Row, London and New York 1961

— *Honest Religion for Secular Man*, SCM Press and Westminster Press, London and Philadelphia 1966

R. K. ORCHARD, *Missions in a Time of Testing*, Lutterworth Press and Westminster Press, London and Philadelphia 1965

K. M. PANIKKAR, *Asia and Western Dominance*, Allen & Unwin and John Day & Co., London and New York 1953

J.-C. PIGUET, *Dieu est mort trois fois*, Cahiers protestants, 6, Lausanne 1966

F. RAAFLAUB, *Mandat sans frontières*, Labor et Fides, Geneva 1965

G. VON RAD, *Old Testament Theology*, trs. D. M. G. Stalker, Oliver & Boyd and Harper & Row, Edinburgh and New York 1962

C. F. RAMUZ, *Œuvres complètes*, 16, Mermod, Lausanne 1941

A. RICH, *Die Weltlichkeit des Glaubens. Diakonie im Horizont der Säkularisierung*, Zwingli Verlag, Zürich-Stuttgart 1966

— *Glaube in politischer Entscheidung*, Zwingli Verlag, Zürich-Stuttgart 1966

J. A. T. ROBINSON, *The New Reformation?*, SCM Press and Westminster Press, London and Philadelphia 1965

The Role of the Diakonia of the Church in Contemporary Society, WCC, Geneva 1966

J. ROSSEL, *Découverte de la mission*, Delachaux et Niestlé, Neuchâtel 1945

H. J. SCHULTZ, *Conversion to the World*, SCM Press and Charles Scribner's Sons, London and New York, 1967

R. SCHUTZ, *Dynamique du provisoire*, Furche Verlag, Taizé 1965

J. V. Taylor, *The Primal Vision*, SCM Press and Fortress Press, London and Philadelphia 1963

Theologische Stimmen aus Asien, Afrika und Latein-Amerika, I, Chr. Kaiser Verlag, Munich 1963

P. Tillich, *Biblical Religion and the Search for Ultimate Reality*, University of Chicago Press, Chicago 1955

Tradition et modernisme en Afrique noire, Editions du Seuil, Paris 1965

United Nations, *Conseils à l'intention des consultants internationaux*, New York 1965

W. A. Visser 't Hooft, *No Other Name*, SCM Press and Westminster Press, London and Philadelphia 1963

— *L'Eglise face au syncretisme*, Labor et Fides, Geneva 1964

E. de Vries, *Man in Rapid Social Change*, SCM Press and Doubleday & Co., London and New York 1961

— (Ed.), *Man in Community*, SCM Press and Association Press, London and New York 1966

T. Wieser (Ed.), *Planning for Mission*, Epworth Press, London 1966

— *Witness in Six Continents*, Edinburgh House Press, London 1964

O. Wolff, *Christus unter den Hindus*, Gerd Mohn, Gütersloh 1965

— *World Conference on Church and Society*, WCC, Geneva 1967

Index

3500,/9